W9-AQU-284

MAN AND TEMPLE

MAN AND TEMPLE

In Ancient Jewish Myth and Ritual

RAPHAEL PATAI

Second Enlarged Edition with a New Introduction and Postscript

KTAV PUBLISHING HOUSE, INC.
NEW YORK

First published 1947

Library of Congress Catalogue Card No. 6722754
Manufactured in United States of America

CONTENTS

TEXT REFERENCES

The numerical references in the text are to notes placed at the ends of the respective chapters

NOTE
ON TEXTS IN RABBINIC LITERATURE

Rabbinic literature is a general term covering the literary works enumerated below :

Mishnah. The basic code of oral tradition collected in its extant form by Rabbi Jehudah the Patriarch in Galilee, *c*. 200 C.E. To the Mishnah were later attached as complementary texts the much larger collections of the Babylonian and Palestinian Talmuds respectively.

Tosefta. A work contemporaneous with the Mishnah, in many respects parallel to it, but containing much additional material, variations from and amplifications of the Mishnah.

Talmud. The name of two large collections containing the discussions of the great Palestinian and Babylonian schools on topics mainly contained in the Mishnah. The *Palestinian Talmud* (also called *Talmud Yerushalmi*—that is, Jerusalem Talmud) reached its final shape in the schools of Galilee about the end of the fourth century C.E. *The Babylonian Talmud*, more bulky, was closed about a century later in Babylonia.

Midrash. A generic term for literary works based upon biblical passages. They fall under two headings, Halakhic and Aggadic Midrashim :

Halakhic Midrashim are primarily interpretations of the laws of the Pentateuch, and comprise works such as the Mekhiltha, Siphra, Siphre, Midrash Haggadol, etc.

Aggadic Midrashim aim at religious and moral instruction, though formally their expositions are attached to passages of the Scripture. To this group belong the Midrash Rabbah (Gen. Rab., Ex. Rab., etc.), Pesiqta di Rabh Kahana, Pesiqta Rabbati, Tanhuma, etc.

In period of time the Midrashim range from the second century C.E. to the Middle Ages.

The translations of the Hebrew and Aramaic texts are mine, with the following exceptions :

The Bible : Authorized Version, with amendments where it seemed necessary

Apocrypha and Pseudepigraphia : Charles' edition

Babylonian Talmud : the translations of those tractates available in Epstein's English edition (London, Soncino Press) were largely followed

ABBREVIATIONS

B.—The Babylonian Talmud, quoted by tractate, folio and page, *e.g.* B. Suk. 43a—Babylonian Talmud, tractate Sukkah, folio 43, page a.

Gen. Rab.—Midrash Genesis (*Berēshith*) Rabbah, quoted by chapter and paragraph, and the pages of Theodor-Albeck's edition, Berlin, 1912–1931, *e.g.* Gen. Rab. 78, 16, p. 936—Genesis Rabbah, chapter 78, paragraph 16, ed. Theodor-Albeck, p. 936. Cf. also Rab.

M.—Mishnah, quoted by tractate, chapter and paragraph, *e.g.* M. Tamid 3, 2.

Rab.—Following the name of one of the five books of the Pentateuch (Gen., Ex., Lev., Num., Deut.) or one of the five Scrolls (*Megilloth*, Cant., Ruth, Thren., Eccl., Esth.)—the Midrash Rabbah to these books, quoted by chapter and paragraph of the Romm, Wilna, edition, *e.g.* Ex. Rab. 15, 22. Cf. also Gen. Rab.

Tos.—Tosefta, quoted by tractate, chapter and paragraph, and the pages of Zuckermandel's edition, Pasewalk, 1881, *e.g.* Tos. Suk. 4, 5, p. 198—Tosefta Sukkah, chapter 4, paragraph 5, ed. Zuckermandel, p. 198.

Y.—*Yerushalmi*, the Jerusalem, or better, the Palestinian Talmud, quoted by tractate, page and column of the Venetian edition, 1523.

THE TRANSCRIPTIONS OF HEBREW WORDS

Because of technical difficulties over the special letters used in Hebrew and other Semitic languages, a rough Anglicized transcription of them has been used for Semitic words quoted in this book

INTRODUCTION

TOWARD the end of 1947, shortly after the publication of the first edition of *Man and Temple* (which, incidentally, was my first book in English, all my previous books having been written in Hebrew), I received a letter whose contents both surprised and delighted me and which first initiated correspondence, then a friendship, and finally collaboration between me and its writer, Robert Graves.

"Dear Mr. Patai," it began, "I have just read your beautifully argued but too brief *Man and Temple.* Do you recall the water sacrifice at Anaphe mentioned in Ap. Rhodius's Argonautica IV 1717 ff? There you have just the same ceremony as at the Tabernacles, including the lightheadedness, in a ritual which was probably Minoan." The letter went on in this vein, with two closely written pages of references, bits of information and detail after fascinating detail of which Graves was reminded, as well as surmises of connections between the Hebrew and the Greek worlds to which he was led through reading my book.

After answering the letter, I placed it in a special file (which was to grow more and more bulky as the years went by), and there it remained until a few months ago, when I began preparations for a new edition of *Man and Temple.* On one of my periodic visits to that greatest of facilities for scholarly research, the New York Public Library, I looked up the passage in the *Argonautica,* and as I thus immersed myself into a renewed study of matters covered in my book, I was carried back in time, not to the Greek world of a remote mythical period about which Apollonius wrote, but to the more recent past of some thirty years ago when I first began the investigations which led to the writing of *Man and Temple.* In those days, I used to work in another library, that of the Hebrew University on Mount Scopus, overlooking the Old City of Jerusalem. And I remembered how often in my excitement, grappling with the meaning of the greatest of ancient Jewish Temple festivals, I would leap from my desk and step over to the window—usually wide open—to feast my eyes on the actual view of the place in which the ancient Temple once stood. There, across the Kidron Valley which separated Mount Scopus from Mount Zion, in a south-south-westerly direction, on the left of the magnificent panorama of Old and New Jerusalem, and looking much nearer than the distance of a little over a mile that actually separated me from it, there rose in serene beauty the Dome of the Rock, built by the Muslim conquerors of Jerusalem upon the same Sacred Rock, the Stone of Foundation, which from the days of Solomon to those of Nebuchadnezzar, and then again from the times of Ezra to those of Titus, bore the Holy of Holies of the Jerusalem Temple.

Closing my eyes for a moment over Apollonius's *Argonautica,* I remembered a still earlier occasion, a day in the summer of 1933, when my friend Shaykh Ahmed F. Al-Kinani first took me into the very midst of those hallowed precincts, up the steps from the narrow shaded and arched streets of the Old City of Jerusalem into the bright, sunlit, wide-open *Haram* court. As soon as we stepped out of the gateway and went up the steps of the Temple platform, there was in front of us, at the surprisingly short distance of some fifty feet, the Dome itself, that most celebrated masterpiece of early Arab architecture.

At first we circled the entire octagonal structure. Then we entered, and in the semi-darkness, beneath the high dome, I saw before me the large, rough native rock, gradually rising from east to west to a height of about six feet above the floor of the corridor surrounding it. In that direction the Rock measured about forty-three feet, and from south to north, sixty. It was surrounded by a wooden railing, which closely followed its outline, with a break at the south-eastern corner, where fourteen steps led down into a subterranean cave which was high enough for me to walk about in it upright.

This, then, was that most sacred spot on earth, the Navel of the Earth, the Foundation Stone of the Earth, the highest point on earth, the connecting link between heaven and earth. Here, over this Rock, stood the Ark of the Covenant with its golden Cherubim, surrounded by the walls of the Adytum, the Holy of Holies, into which only the High Priest was allowed to enter, and even he only once a year, on the most solemn Day of Atonement. I spent a long time gazing at the boulder itself, trying to fix into my memory every detail of its rugged, scarred and time-worn face. At the time I knew very little about the Rock, its myths and the rites performed over and around it, but the little I knew suddenly surged in on me in the hushed atmosphere of the Dome, and the primeval, stark, unhewn stone in the midst of the delicate columns of the *Qubba* filled me with awe and curiosity. The old Biblical epithet for God, "Rock of Israel," kept sounding in my ear, and it must have been under the influence of all these factors that I decided—I no longer remember whether then and there or later—to make a study of the ancient Temple of Jerusalem and its associated myths and rituals.

The early results of those studies were incorporated into a paper entitled "The 'Control of Rain' in Ancient Palestine," which was published in Volume XIV of the *Hebrew Union College Annual* (Cincinnati, Ohio, 1939). Thereafter, my attention was drawn to the wider problems of the relationship between man and earth in general, which resulted in the two Hebrew volumes entitled *Adam v'Adama, Man and Earth in Hebrew Custom, Belief and Legend* (Jerusalem, The Hebrew University Press, 1942-43). After the publication of the second book of this study, I felt ready to return to the Jerusalem Temple, and early in 1946 the manuscript of a modest volume on the subject was completed. Through the good offices of my friend Professor H.H. Rowley, it was submitted to Thomas Nelson and Sons Ltd. in Edinburgh, who published it in the summer of 1947.

When reissuing a study after twenty years, several courses are open to the author. One is to bring it up to date by adding the results of relevant researches that have appeared since its publication. I was not able to follow this course because the time that would have been required for such a reworking was prohibitive. The other is to regard the original as a quasi-historical document and leave it unchanged. This, indeed, is what I first intended to do. But upon rereading the book I found that it left unsaid several things for which the foundation was laid in the argument presented in it. I therefore decided to augment the new edition by a Postscript, sketching out some of the additional insights which came to me while reading the book I wrote twenty years earlier. Apart from this new material, and a very few and minor corrections in the body of the text itself, the book has remained unchanged.

Forest Hills, N.Y.
April, 1967

Chapter One

NATURE AND THE SUPERNATURAL

I

Modern researches probing from various angles into the social function of early religions have proved that a main concern of primary religious activities is to obtain and secure the maximum of material welfare for the whole of the community. Much has also been learned about the ways and means resorted to in order to bring about the regular functioning of nature upon which the well-being of man almost exclusively depended. In the ancient Near East, where intricate religious systems were evolved, these ways and means became crystallized into a complex ritual pattern centering round great seasonal festivals. The development of this ritual pattern has been subjected to thorough investigation by a number of scholars, the gist of whose findings Professor S. H. Hooke sums up in the following words :

> The picture which emerges from a study of the great seasonal rituals of the ancient East and their associated myths is that of a community seeking to bring under control by means of an organized system of ritual actions the order of nature upon the functioning of which its well-being depends.[1]

Not only in the great seasonal rituals, but also in many other practices of communal and private life, one could detect the working of the same trend, namely, towards influencing and controlling the order of nature.

Let us take a closer look at the process that may have led up to this " organized system of ritual actions " and to all the other communal and private rituals that abounded in the ancient Near East.

Ever since there emerged on earth that special form of existence which is called human life, its bearer, man, has endeavoured to make life more agreeable and to create for himself more comfortable living conditions. Man evolved tools to make it easier for himself to gather and to produce food, and to make life safer from the attacks of beast and man. He built himself shelters for safety and comfort. He made clothing to guard himself against the rigours of the climate, and applied ornamental embellishments to different parts of his body. He invented and improved methods for the production of food ; he gradually became an expert in one or another special branch of production and developed specialized industries. He evolved various systems of property, stationary and movable, and learned to barter his own superfluous possessions for those of others. He developed regular relationships within smaller and larger human groups ; and by giving more or less fixed forms to these relations in custom and law, he assigned to each individual a place within society circumscribed by special rights and duties.

In all these activities man appeared as a reasonable and rational being, who knew what he wanted and sought ways and means of obtaining it.

But the advantages and benefits man wished to derive from his natural and social environment were by no means of a material nature only, such as would satisfy physical, biological and social needs. The benefits were often psychological, satisfying mental needs having no biological, economic or social foundation, but arising from the special psychical constitution of man. Yet the measures taken to satisfy these mental or psychical needs might be the same as those taken for the satisfaction of the physical, biological and social needs, or at least very similar to them ; and might, and in fact very often did, pertain to concrete natural objects.[2]

Moreover, even in satisfying primary needs arising out of the physical nature of man, the actual practices adopted by him are in the great majority of cases not spontaneous and unpremeditated, but motivated in accordance with mental predilections and inclinations. A survey of the methods followed by various communities in their choice, preparation and consumption of food, as well as in the evaluation of food-stuffs as objects of property, would show what a wide range of difference can be introduced by these mental predilections and inclinations even into the forms of satisfaction of so vital and primary an impulse as hunger.

Thus we see that human actions directed towards natural objects are generated by both physical and psychical necessities. The same two necessities prompt human activities also in relation to the supernatural.

II

The existence of the supernatural in one form or another is taken for granted by all the peoples of the earth, even the most primitive. Though its existence is in most instances somewhat obscure, proved only by what may be called secondary signs, it is nevertheless a certainty and reality. Prehistoric finds bear witness to the fact that already in the Old Stone Age man lived not only in the light of the physical world, but also in the shadow of the supernatural world.

It would be outside our present theme to deal with the extent and content of the supernatural world. Let us state only this : the lower boundary of the supernatural, that which borders upon the natural world, was seldom exactly the same in two different societies, nor was it constant within one and the same society over a considerable period of time. Furthermore, even in the same period and in the same society, different people had different conceptions of the supernatural, as also one and the same man may have in different moods or emotional situations.

Every culture and every cultural stage had its own accumulation of knowledge about the physical world, its own degree of familiarity with natural phenomena, and it was in accordance with this actual knowledge of nature that the borderline between nature and the supernatural had to run. It would, though, be a mistake to suppose that the supernatural had always to be contented with such territories as were left over to it by the natural science of a given people at a certain time. We have rather to imagine a balance being maintained between two mutually active forces. More often than not it was the established view of the supernatural and its working which determined what territories should be left over to practical exploration and scientific investigation.

Lightning, for instance, belonged to the sphere of the supernatural with many ancient peoples, among them Israel and the Greeks. It was believed to be the arrow or the spear of the god. Modern physical science has subjected lightning to investigation and found that it is but an electrical phenomenon obeying certain physical laws. Physicists are even able to engender lightning artificially. Thus the supernatural had to yield this traditional weapon to natural science. Nevertheless, many a simpler folk still regards lightning as a heavenly weapon, and should a wicked man be struck by it, there would be no doubt as to the true significance of the event : a punishment from on high.

All this may seem to imply that there exists a sharply drawn line of demarcation between the natural and the supernatural. But nothing would be falser than such an assumption. Indeed natural and supernatural appear very often as intricately interwoven, and as merely two different aspects of the same object, action or phenomenon. It can even be said that each and every natural object, action or phenomenon may under given circumstances have also a spiritual quality, a supernatural aspect or value.

It is of interest to consider how man succeeded in harnessing for his use the supernatural powers also, or the supernatural aspect of the universe.

The need to do so was bound to arise when man was faced with a situation for which his practical experience proved insufficient. At the time of a crisis in private or communal life man feels that he needs the help of supernatural powers. In danger or in a situation the outcome of which is doubtful, when man, hoping for a certain thing to happen and at the same time fearing lest another thing might happen, has no power to influence the oncoming event by the usual *natural* means, he tries to realize his wish, and to prevent the unwanted, by applying to the supernatural for help. Thus Malinowski observed relative to practices in the Trobriand Islands:

> It is most significant that in the lagoon fishing, where man can rely completely upon his knowledge and skill, magic does not exist, while in the open-sea fishing, full of danger and uncertainty, there is extensive magical ritual to secure safety and good results.[3]

In the great majority of his undertakings primitive man is faced by two sets of problems. The one, the predictable and controllable, he can overcome with technical skill ; the second, the unpredictable and uncontrollable, he tries to solve by this appeal to the supernatural. And just as the technical methods are never an improvisation but an application of well-tried ways and means, so the appeal to the supernatural too tends to assume fixed forms, and when often repeated—and especially when recurring seasonally—it becomes a rite, or, if more complex, a ritual.

Generally speaking, the less developed a community, the simpler its technology and poorer its civilizatory equipment, the greater will be the role played by the unpredictable and uncontrollable element in its life, and consequently the greater the importance of the function of the ritual directed towards the control of the elusive forces. Among primitive peoples almost everything has its ritual, every undertaking, every action and every event, down to such minute affairs as plucking a fruit or sitting down to rest. Among more advanced peoples only the more significant events in private and communal life retain their ritual, and among the peoples of modern western civilization ritual has almost entirely lost its significance, surviving only in occasional ceremonies of church and state.

III

Before coming to the actual procedure of what we called the "appeal to the supernatural," we have first of all to acquaint ourselves with the main principle on which are based most, if not all, the attempts of primitive man at influencing nature. For, paradoxical as it may sound, most of the practices of primitive man in which the supernatural is resorted to are intended to influence the elements and phenomena of nature only.

Without entering into the problems presented by the various forms of outlook on nature, such as mana, pre-animism or animatism, animism and the personification and symbolical representation of natural forces and elements, let us state in brief that the common denominator of these different concepts is the assumption of a basic similarity between man and the other parts of nature. According to this assumption all the elements, parts, powers and phenomena of nature partake of "human nature." Popular imagination does not find it difficult to endow the component parts of nature even with human forms, but more often it is the inner constitution, the mental make-up of man, that is attributed to all parts of animate and inanimate nature. The Indians of Guiana, for instance, do not draw "any sharp line of distinction, such as we see between animals—man included—and inanimate objects. On the contrary, to the Indian all objects, animate and inanimate, seem exactly of the same nature, except that they differ in the accident of bodily form. . . ."[4]

The fact that primitive man draws no strict line of cleavage between the animal, vegetable and mineral kingdoms on the one hand, and human beings on the other, has been so often emphasized that it can be regarded as an anthropological commonplace.[5] Westermarck has adduced evidence to show that the primitive belief in the similarity between the lower animals and man is to be found again among the peoples of classical antiquity, those of the Middle Ages, and the simpler folk in modern civilized countries.[6] Elsewhere we have had occasion to show that the same concept was prevalent also among the ancient Hebrews both in biblical and in post-biblical times.[7]

For our present purpose it will be sufficient to stress only one detail in this general conception of "humanized" nature, namely, that which endows the heavenly bodies, the sun, moon and stars, with a nature and consciousness akin to man's own. Again, it will be unnecessary to attest with examples that among many primitive peoples these heavenly bodies are regarded as human beings, the sun as a man, the moon as a woman, or vice versa ; and that by these peoples the stars too "are not merely talked of in fancied personality, but personal action is attributed to them."[8] It is well known that among many primitive peoples, as well as among the civilized peoples of antiquity, among them the early Hebrews, the heavenly bodies were not only personified but regarded as deities and as such revered and worshipped.[9] What is perhaps less well known is the significant fact that in later Jewish thought the heavenly bodies, though naturally no longer regarded as deities, were still looked upon as beings of human and even superhuman intelligence. According to Philo Judaeus (born *circa* 20–10 B.C.) the stars stand even higher than the angels, in fact they are the highest class or degree of the cosmos ; they are eternal living beings who populate the heavens, and possess both soul and mind. Philo calls them " majestic, divine, soulful beings," or, leaning upon Pythagorean-Platonic ideas, even " gods perceptible by the senses."[10]

Exactly the same ideas about the human and superhuman nature of the heavenly bodies are found again in post-biblical Jewish literature. Ever since the creation of man, according to Jewish legend, the heavenly bodies have had ample opportunity to intervene in human affairs. There were occasions, it is true, when they showed themselves hostile to man, but in general their interventions were prompted by sympathy and kindness.[11] The concept that the heavenly bodies are beings similar to man in their mental make-up, but endowed with superhuman intelligence, was taught also by Arab and Jewish philosophers in the Middle Ages. Maimonides (A.D. 1135–1204) said : " All the stars and spheres have souls, intelligence and understanding. They are living and they endure and recognize Him who created the world by His word. Each one of them according to its rank and status praises and worships its Maker just as the angels do. And just as they know the Holy One, blessed be He, so they know themselves and know the angels who stand above them. And the understanding of the stars and spheres is smaller than that of the angels, but greater than that of man." [12]

Hymns containing this concept are to be found in Jewish prayer-books to this day. In the Sabbath morning prayer the following passage occurs :

> Good are the luminaries which our God created. He made them to have knowledge, understanding and wisdom. He has endued them with power and might to be rulers in the world. They are full of splendour and radiate brightness, their splendour is graceful throughout the world. They rejoice when going forth and are glad at their return, they do with awe the will of their Creator. They give glory and honour to His name, joy and song to the memory of His kingdom.[13]

But to return to primitive peoples, to their outlook on nature and to the ways and means resorted to by them in their " appeal to the supernatural." We have seen that by simply attributing to nature human properties, primitive man has endowed nature with what in our view appears as a supernatural quality, but what is to him merely a recognition of the true state of things, the perception of the fundamental similarity underlying the apparent diversity of forms. This basic outlook on the spiritual homogeneity of all existing things has its analogy in the modern scientific approach to the physical world, discerning behind the great variety of elements the same ultimate components, the protons and electrons.

IV

Homogeneity in spiritual quality means not only a structural but also a functional similarity. As Hartland has remarked, " The external world is first interpreted by the savage thinker in the terms of his own consciousness."[14] The natives of Central Borneo, for instance, "regard themselves as not essentially but only in degree different from the animals, plants and stones of their environment. Characteristically the Bahau ascribe not only to themselves but also to all animate and inanimate beings the possession of souls. According to their opinion, the soul of a tree, a dog or a rock, reacts in the same way as the soul of man and is moved by the same feelings of pleasure and pain. . . ."[15]

This essential similarity between man and the other parts of nature implies not only a similarity in reactions and feelings, but also the possibility of influencing all parts of nature by the same means and methods that have proved successful in social intercourse among human beings. This personalistic interpretation of nature, well attested in numerous primitive societies, extends the limits of society to include nature as a whole.[16] According to the Kpelle, for instance, "man, living or dead, demons, animals, plants and inanimate objects are essentially the same, and exist under similar conditions; they can in the same way influence man towards good or evil, they all can be either harmful or useful to him, and on the other hand he can influence them because they are all similar to him."[17] In other words, just as man is able to influence his fellow-men by words, signs or actions, within an ordered and properly functioning society, so he can do with nature. He can make his fellow-man do his will by begging, coaxing, commanding, bribing or forcing him, and the same methods hold good also with nature. In addition to this, if he wants to achieve his end in society, he has to obey certain rules of conduct which often impose on him considerable discomfort, and similarly if he wants to be successful in his dealings with nature he has to perform certain actions bearing the same general character as his actions in respect to his fellow-men, both assuming on certain important occasions a ritual character. In short, the rules of active and passive conduct, well tried and proven in society, hold good—according to this concept—in nature also ; nature is conceived of as a part of society, subject to the same rules of sympathy which govern society.

Since examples to illustrate this social attitude of man on a primitive level towards objects of nature abound in anthropological literature, it does not seem necessary to repeat any of them here.[18] We need but refer to that general type of rite in which man endeavours to ensure the fertility of plants, trees or fields by the simple method of resorting to the same acts as would cause the fertilization of women, or by enacting the ceremonies that in human relations usually precede the sexual connection, namely, the marriage ceremonies.[19] In other instances the growth of certain plants, regarded as personal beings, is promoted not by sexual acts but by oral influence, by persuasion and requests.[20]

Addressing objects of nature, such as the heavenly bodies, the wind, the rain, the waters, the mountains, the trees, and so on, as reasonable beings and asking them to do this or that for the sake of man, is a method of influencing nature widely prevalent among primitive peoples both with or without the accompaniment of corresponding acted rites or ceremonies. It is not necessary to rely exclusively upon the concept of the "power of the word" so ably demonstrated by Ernest Crawley[21] for the explanation of the rites in which man endeavours to influence nature by word of mouth. In many cases, when the words expressing the wish are repeated many times the impression is quite clearly not that of delivering a command but that of putting forward a request, or, in other words, not that of magic control but that of social persuasion.

In rain-making ceremonies it is an almost universal feature that the request for rain, expressed in short sentences like "Rain, come!" or "Rains, fall!" and the like, is repeated hundreds of times, until either rain comes or the performers have to stop out of sheer exhaustion. This certainly is much closer to the behaviour of the poor beggar who ceaselessly repeats his humble request for alms, than to the action of the powerful rich man who has only to say the word and the amount needed by him is put at his disposal.

It is this sort of request mingled with persuasion that could without any strain or shock be transferred from being directed to the entities of nature to being addressed to the ruler over nature, God. It is, moreover, only this same sort of *dromenon*, thing enacted, aimed at a quasi-social persuasion by showing what is desired of nature, which could survive in the form of complementary rites in public and official religious ritual directed towards a deity of the highest metaphysical quality. Rites aiming at the direct magical control of nature would have been essentially contradictory to the service of such a deity, and could scarcely have appeared in his temple-festivities hand in hand with prayers and supplicatory sacrifices. Divine service could, on the other hand, tolerate with some generosity supplication and persuasion directed to the lesser powers in nature, which, according to the religious conception, were subservient to God alone.

V

The question now arises, what has this quasi-social persuasion of the natural forces, elements and objects to do with the " appeal to the supernatural," which, as stated above, is a method complementary to, but distinct from, the practical steps undertaken by man to achieve certain concrete results? In fact, it is time to rectify and amend. When we said " appeal to the supernatural " we applied one of our categories to primitive mentality, in relation to which, strictly speaking, such categories are not applicable. When a savage prepares his garden, plants his fruit-tree, waters it, weeds it, and also executes high jumps and calls " grow high, grow high ! " in order to " make " the plant grow high, and lays heavy stones at its foot in order to "make" its fruit heavy, we feel that he uses in his gardening two fundamentally different procedures, the one based on practical knowledge, the other on supernatural influences. For the savage gardener himself no such distinction exists. He merely executes a series of actions all of which are necessary in one and the same degree in order to make the plant thrive. Let us not forget that for him the plant is a living being, very near to himself in substance and quality. He prepares the land and waters the plant just as he would prepare a comfortable couch and procure food for his child. And just as he would tell or show his child whatever he would wish him to do or to be, so he tells and shows the plant what he wishes it to do and to be: to grow high and to be heavy with fruit. From the point of view of the savage there is actually nothing supernatural in the whole procedure; he deals with a natural object, which has to undergo a natural process, in accordance with the natural properties he knows it to possess. But this natural object, like each and every object existing in the world, has also a spiritual quality. So he utters words and executes actions appropriate to the occasion and apt to influence the spiritual side of the plant.

VI

If this be so, another question will probably be asked. If the "appeal to the supernatural" was just a part of the natural dealing with the natural elements and objects, a sort of social approach to their spiritual side, why did it, after all, become in almost every society the special field of activity of one or another type of " religious " authority, such as the magician, the diviner, the priest or the prophet ?

The specialization in the " supernatural " cannot be regarded as a phenomenon *sui generis*. It should be viewed as one instance of the general trend of occupational specialization which sets in everywhere when a certain level of cultural development is reached. When metal tools begin to be used, the average agriculturist does not find it practicable any more to make for himself his own tools as he did so long as the tools were of stone or flint. The community delegates one of its sons for the performance of the task that has grown too complicated. As soon as one of the community undertakes to be the smith and to supply all the others with tools, he by sheer routine develops his work until soon it grows so specialized, refined and complicated by innumerable tricks of the trade as entirely to surpass the products of the unpractised skill of the simple food collector or producer.

Thus too the " appeal to the supernatural." To deal with the inner, hidden qualities of the objects of nature required a special technique which, growing too cumbersome for the average hunter or agriculturist, became entrusted to the hands of a specialist who performed the necessary ceremonies for any individual layman or for the community as a whole. And once in the hands of a specialist, the rites began to increase in both volume and intricacy, ever more and more stress being laid on accuracy in rendering the oral parts of the rites and on precision in performing the *dromena*, the things done. The knowledge of rituals, especially that of the great seasonal rites, soon withdrew far beyond the reach of the average laymen whose participation in the life-giving performance became confined to secondary mass-roles following the instructions of the few privileged principals. The task of the primitive " divine " thus came to be recognized as that of dealing with the supernatural, and his profession became in many a society the first or even the only specialized work.

VII

In the foregoing very sketchy presentation of a cultural process we have endeavoured to deal only with that aspect of the supernatural which can be interpreted as the spiritual side of nature and its component parts. We have not touched upon those vast realms of the supernatural which human phantasy peopled with spiritual beings conceived as independent of any natural or physical form. Nor does our delineation lay claim to general validity. Cultural development followed everywhere its own way, and it would be futile to contend that the evolution of ritual and priesthood was the result of a process common to all the peoples of the world.

We have emphasized the social aspect of man's approach to the forces of nature not only because another aspect, the magical control of nature, has been only too often stressed and overstressed by many an anthropological writer, but also, and chiefly, because it seems to us that in many cases it is precisely this social approach that has left its trace on the outlook on nature as well as on the myth and ritual of the ancient Hebrews in biblical and post-biblical times. And it is with the relation of man and nature as reflected in ancient Jewish myth and ritual that the present study deals.

Professor Kelsen in a recent book has shown that primitive man sees in the working of nature the manifestation of the "principle of retribution."[22] Primitive man (and to a great extent also a community as advanced as the ancient Greeks), interpreting nature according to social norms, found the *lex talionis*, the norm of retribution, the biblical "an eye for an eye," not only in society but also in nature. In the following pages we shall try to show that other parallels, too, exist in what may be more comprehensively called "the law of sympathy in nature." The material we shall make use of will be drawn mainly from literary sources relating to the closing period of the Second Temple in Jerusalem.

Popular conceptions are not very easily discernible in the talmudic and midrashic literature originating in the first centuries of the Christian era. The sages of the Talmud who constitute the literary and religious sieve through which popular traditions had to pass before entering the rich granaries of ancient Jewish literature, withheld many a grain of coarser quality and let through others only in a broken-up form or reduced size. The age, too, an age of turmoil, of political upheavals and national revolts, of philosophical innovations and new religious messages, was most unfavourable to the conservation of old popular traditions. If, in spite of all these adverse factors, so much of the popular traditional material gained access to those literary granaries, it was mainly due to two facts. First, much of what was originally folk-lore had become in the course of time sanctified and had grown to be inseparable from other items of religion of a quite different origin. Second, everyday life, of which much is recorded in ancient Jewish literature, was thoroughly permeated by popular traditions, customs, habits and usages. Be this as it may, the fact is that talmudic and midrashic literature constitutes a veritable storehouse for the folk-lorist and the cultural anthropologist. This material, though much richer than that contained in the earlier biblical and apocryphal literature, is far less easily accessible to students of anthropology, since it is written partly in Hebrew, partly in Aramaic, and partly in a mixture of both, and is translated only incompletely into European languages (mainly into German).

In these pages we should like to choose out of this rich material a few illustrations of the working of the principle of sympathy in nature as revealed in such diverse forms as rituals performed in the Second

Temple of Jerusalem, myths centering around this Temple, and beliefs concerning the conduct and actions of the people in general and of the children, the rulers, and the pious and righteous men in particular.

1 S. H. Hooke, in *The Labyrinth*, London, 1935, pp. 213 sqq.
2 B. Malinowski, *Argonauts of the Western Pacific*, London, 1922, p. 89.
3 B. Malinowski, "Magic, Science and Religion," in *Science, Religion and Reality*, ed. by Joseph Needham, New York, 1925, p. 32.
4 E. F. im Thurn, *Among the Indians of Guiana*, 1883, pp. 350 sq.
5 E. S. Hartland, *The Legend of Perseus*, London, 1894–96, vol. I, pp. 207 sq., and *Primitive Paternity*, London, 1909–10, vol. I, pp. 191, 246, 250 ; E. B. Tylor, *Primitive Culture*, 4th ed., London, 1903, vol. I, pp. 467 sq. ; James G. Frazer, *The Golden Bough*, 2nd ed., vol. II, pp. 389 sqq., and *Folk-lore in the Old Testament*, London, 1919, vol. III, pp. 415 sqq. ; F. Liebrecht, *Zur Volkskunde*, Heilbronn, 1879, p. 17.
6 E. Westermarck, *The Origin and Development of the Moral Ideas*, London, 1906–26, vol. I, pp. 252 sqq.
7 Raphael Patai, *Man and Earth in Hebrew Custom, Belief and Legend, A Study in Comparative Religion* (in Hebrew), Jerusalem, 1942–43, vol. I, pp. 23 sqq.
8 Tylor, *Primitive Culture*, vol. I, p. 290, cf. also pp. 288 sqq.
9 Frazer, *The Worship of Nature*, London, 1926, vol. I, pp. 441 sqq. ; Hastings' *Encyclopaedia of Religion and Ethics*, vol. XII, pp. 48 sqq. ; D. Nielsen, *Die altarabische Mondreligion und die mosaische Überlieferung*, Strassburg, 1904 ; W. Robertson Smith, *The Religion of the Semites*, 3rd ed. by S. A. Cook, London, 1927, pp. 134 sq., 542, 649 sq., 669, 672 ; J. Morgenstern, "The Gates of Righteousness," *Hebrew Union College Annual*, VI (1929), pp. 1 sqq. ; A. Lods, *Israel*, Paris, 1932, Index, s.v. lune,

soleil ; F. J. Hollis, "The Sun-Cult and the Temple at Jerusalem," in *Myth and Ritual*, ed. S. H. Hooke, Oxford, 1933, pp. 87 sqq. ; Oesterley and Robinson, *Hebrew Religion*, 2nd ed., London, 1937, Index, s.v. Moon, Stars, Sun ; W. F. Albright, *Archaeology and the Religion of Israel*, Baltimore, 1942, p. 167.

10 Philo Judaeus, *de specialibus legibus*, I, 13 ; *de gigantibus*, 7 ; *de aeternitate mundi*, 45, 47 ; *de somniis*, I, 22, 34, 135 ; *de opificio mundi*, 27, 73 ; *de plantatione*, 12 ; *de Abrahamo*, 165 ; *legum alleg*. II, 10 ; *quis rerum div. heres sit*, 75 ; cf. Helmut Schmidt, *Die Anthropologie Philons von Alexandrien*, Würzburg (1934), p. 27 ; A. Aptowitzer, "The Rewarding and Punishing of Animals and Inanimate Objects," *Hebrew Union College Annual*, III (1926), p. 147.

11 Vita Adae et Evae, 36 ; Tanhuma Numeri, ed. Buber, p. 94 ; cf. B. Sanhedrin, 110a. More details see Patai, *Man and Earth*, vol. I, pp. 47 sqq.

12 Maimonides, *Mishne Torah*, part I, Yesode Torah, 3, 9, and cf. *The Guide of the Perplexed*, II, ch. 4.

13 Daily Prayers, New York, 1938, with English translation, pp. 350 sq.

14 Hartland, *Ritual and Belief*, London, 1914, p. 27.

15 A. W. Nieuwenhuis, *Quer durch Borneo*, 1904, I, 96. Quoted by Kelsen, *Society and Nature*, Chicago, 1943, p. 7.

16 Cf. Kelsen, *Society and Nature*, Chicago, 1943, p. vii.

17 D. Westermann, *Die Kpelle*, Göttingen, 1921, p. 174.

18 Kelsen, *Society and Nature*, Chicago, 1943, ch. X, § 10 : "Actual Behaviour of Early Man Toward Objects of Nature," pp. 31 sqq.

19 Cf., for instance, Frazer, *The Golden Bough*, 3rd ed., I, 40 ; II, 57, 100 sq., 316 ; also his *Aftermath*, pp. 153 sq. ; *Folk-lore*, vii (1896), p. 206 ; E. Crawley, *The Mystic Rose*, London, 1927, vol. II, pp. 55 sqq. ; Richard Schmidt, *Liebe und Ehe im alten und modernen Indien*, Berlin, 1904, p. 406 ; B. Nyberg, *Kind und Erde*, Helsingfors, 1931, pp. 199 sq. ; W. Crook, *The Native Races of the British Empire*, VI, *Natives of Northern India*, London,

1907, II, 115 sq. ; E. Westermarck, *The History of Human Marriage*, London, 1921, vol. II, pp. 523 sqq. ; E. Lehman, in Chantepie de la Saussaye, *Lehrbuch der Religionsgeschichte*, Tübingen, 1925, vol. I, p. 41, etc.

20 So, for instance, among the natives of Dobu, cf. R. F. Fortune, *Sorcerers of Dobu*, 1932, pp. 94 sqq., 97, 101 sq., 107 sqq.

21 E. Crawley, *Oath, Curse and Blessing*, Thinker's Library, No. 40, London, 1934, pp. 1 sqq. ; as to the ancient Jewish belief in the power of the word, cf. Patai, *Man and Earth*, vol. II, pp. 272 sqq.

22 H. Kelsen, *Society and Nature*, Chicago, 1943.

Chapter Two

THE RITUAL OF WATER-LIBATION

I

The most elaborate yearly ritual performed in the Second Temple of Jerusalem was one neither prescribed nor even mentioned in the Bible. It is the so-called "Joy of the House of Water Drawing"[1] to which a traditional setting was given by connecting it with the Feast of Tabernacles.[2] This feast was celebrated at the beginning of the Hebrew year, in the autumn, at the time when in Palestine the rainy season is about to begin.[3]

The festivities drew a large crowd to the Temple Mount. The people were kept busy day and night attending various ceremonies and public performances during the seven or eight days of the festival. On the first day of the feast they rose early in the morning to be present at the offering of the daily morning sacrifice which was slaughtered ere the sun rose.[4] After that they went to attend prayers at one of the synagogues that in the last decades of the Second Temple already abounded in Jerusalem. From the prayer back to the Temple to attend the Mussaf, the additional sacrifice of the feast, then again to the Mussaf-prayers. These over, some went to the School of the Law, while others felt the urge to offer up private vows and alms. Thus noon arrived, when people would go to have their meals, after which again back to the school, to the study of the Law, until the Minha, the afternoon prayer and the daily sacrifice of twilight.[5] Immediately following these began the festivities of the Joy of the House of Water-Drawing, which lasted until the following morning when the water-libation (see below) took place.[6] This full programme of twenty-four hours was repeated during each of the seven days of the feast. And since it is impossible, as one of the sages remarks, for a human being to exist without sleep for several consecutive days, they used to slumber for short intervals each on the shoulder of his friend.[7]

But these were by no means all the duties the participants had to perform. Every day, with the exception of the Sabbath, they went down to the village of Motza, some three to four miles west of Jerusalem, called in those days also Kalonia, *i.e.* Colonia,[8] and gathered there willow branches each at least eleven cubits long, *i.e.* about five and a half yards. These branches, which had to be soft and flexible, were placed in a perpendicular position around the altar so that their tops would be bent over the altar itself.[9] When the altar was thus covered with a green coating the shofar horn was sounded: a *teqi'ah*, a long blast, a *teru'ah*, a tremulous blast, and again a *teqi'ah*, and the circumambulation of the altar began. This was done once every day accompanied by such cries as "O God, help us; O God, give us luck."[10] On the seventh day they went round the altar seven times, and upon taking leave of the altar they cried, " Beauty hast thou, O altar ! beauty hast thou, O altar ! "

On this seventh day another rite was performed—a highly significant one as we shall later see—with palm twigs, or, according to another version, with willow branches. Such smaller branches were brought along and the festive throng beat them upon the altar.[11] This rite even gave the day its name : The Day of Branch-Beating (or of Willow-Beating). During every circumambulation each of the participants held his *lulab* in his hands. The lulab consisted, as it does to this day, of a long thin palm branch and some smaller branches of willow and myrtle tied together, used in conjunction with a citron, the so-called ethrog. This lulab was also carried along by each male wherever he went during all the seven days of the feast with the exception of the Sabbath. After the branch-beating on the seventh day the children used to throw away the lulabs and to eat the ethrogs.[12]

Since on the Sabbath the general prohibition of carrying anything prevented the people from carrying their lulabs to the Temple, special arrangements were made. The lulabs were carried beforehand on the Friday to the Temple Mount, where the attendants of the Temple received the branches from their hands and arrayed them on shelves.[13] Before the people left the place they were instructed to say, " Whosoever gets my lulab in his hands, let it be his as a gift." This was necessary, as the use of a borrowed or a stolen lulab was ritually forbidden. Next day, on the Sabbath, the courts of the Temple witnessed a tumultuous scene. As the masses of the people arrived, the attendants threw the lulabs among them and each one did his best to catch one of the flying branches, the struggle invariably ending in blows. When the *Bēth Din*, the Law Court, saw that these proceedings involved danger, they ordained that on the Sabbath each one should use his lulab only at his home.[14]

II

Let us now return to the first day of the festival, or rather to its first night. Towards evening, at the close of the first day of the feast, began the " Joy of the House of Water-Drawing." This was the most magnificent and joyous festival of the whole Jewish ritual year. The description of this festival, contained in the Mishnah, opens with the following words : " Whosoever has not seen the Joy of the House of Water-Drawing has never seen real joy in his life."[15] The festivities began with a precautionary measure. Originally during the festivities women used to stand within the great courtyard called the Women's Court, which was the scene of the festivals, while the men were without. But the two sexes used to intermingle and to commit what is euphemistically called *qaluth rōsh*, " lightheadedness." The sages first ordained that the men and women should change places, but still " lightheadedness " occurred. Then the sages, having had special galleries built round about three sides of the courtyard, ordered the women to sit in them, in order to prevent the people from giving way to the temptation of the " evil inclination " that overpowers man in the hour of joy.[16]

When the day grew dark the great candelabra were lighted. Each of these tall golden lampstands carried on its top four bowls which had to be filled with oil.[17] Four ladders were placed against the four branches of the candelabra, and up them climbed four of the priestly youths called in Hebrew "the Flowers of Priesthood." In their hands they carried pitchers to fill the bowls.[18] Wicks for the outer lamps were made of the worn-out drawers and girdles of the priests, while the wicks of the inner lamps were made of the drawers of the High Priest.[19] The light shed by these high lamps was so great that the whole of Jerusalem was lit up by it, and, as it is specially recorded, women could sift wheat by this illumination.[20]

One must suppose that these preparations took considerable time. In the meantime spirits rose higher and higher until the " pious men " and the " men of [good] deeds," whose great hour this was, began to dance before the people with burning torches in their hands.[21] It is told of the venerable Rabban Shimeon ben Gamliel himself, that he used to dance with eight golden burning torches ; he threw them high up into the air and again caught them alternately, and so great was his skill that no torch ever touched another nor did any torch ever fall to earth. Nay, even more than that, Rabban Shimeon ben Gamliel could perform, alone of all men, the following form of prostration : he threw himself forward upon his face, supported himself for a moment with his two thumbs stuck to the floor, kissed the floor and immediately jumped back to standing position.[22] Other sages performed similar feats and entertained the audience with enigmatic sayings.[23]

In the meantime the Levites took up positions upon the fifteen steps leading from the Women's Court to the inner Court of the Israelites, the floor of which lay some yards higher. In their hands were harps, lyres, cymbals, trumpets and numerous other musical instruments, and they began to sing, accompanying themselves.[24] They sang the so-called fifteen "Songs of Ascents" contained in the book of Psalms.[25] The fifteen steps, the Mishnah expressly states, corresponded to the fifteen Songs of Ascents.[26]

While the greater part of the night was thus spent in singing, playing and dancing, two priests stood high above the humming crowd, at the upper gate which led from the Court of the Israelites down to the Women's Court. In their hands they held trumpets and they stood listening for the first crowing of the cock. As soon as they heard the cock crow they immediately lifted their trumpets to their lips and blew a triple blast, *teqi'ah*, *teru'ah*, *teqi'ah*.[27] These sounds were a signal for the cessation of the merriment. The crowd arrayed itself in the wake of the priests to descend in procession to the well of

Siloam. The procession, which went out through the eastern Water-Gate,[28] moved slowly, and was often brought to a standstill by repeated trumpet-blasts. When they reached the Water-Gate the people turned back towards the west, facing the Sanctuary, and solemnly declared :

> Our fathers who were on this place [stood] with their backs towards the Sanctuary and their faces towards the east, and they prostrated themselves eastwards to the sun.[29] But as for us, our eyes are turned to the Lord.[30]

Then the procession moved on, and when it reached the Siloam the priest who was charged with drawing the water from the well filled his golden pitcher, after which the whole procession returned the way it had come. When again reaching the inner courtyard, the priest mounted the ramp leading from the south side up to the altar, and poured the water into one of the two bowls that were placed there for the purpose. These two bowls were made of silver, or, according to another version, out of lime. Into the bowl on the western side the priest had to pour the water brought from the Siloam, while the eastern bowl was to receive a libation of wine. But as it often happened that the priest erred and interchanged the two liquids, both bowls became with time blackened by the thick red wine of Palestine, until their material became unrecognizable.[31] The libation of three " log," *i.e.* about one and a half litres, of water, and the same amount of wine was repeated during each of the seven days of the feast.[32]

The bottom of each bowl had a perforated spout

to let the liquid out, and before the priest performed the act of libation he stopped these up with corks. Then he poured the water and the wine into the respective bowls, and afterwards removed both corks simultaneously. In order that the thick wine should take exactly the same time to flow down as the much thinner water, the hole of the wine-bowl was made larger than that of the water-bowl. The water flowed down into the *shitin*, the perpendicular shafts underneath the altar, of the rich mythical connotations of which we shall later hear more, while the wine flowed into a small passage-way or vat which was situated to the south-west of the altar.[33] Once every sixty or seventy years priestly children descended into this vat to collect the congealed wine which accumulated there in a form resembling dried rounds of pressed figs, and burned it in a state of sanctity, that is, in a holy place in the Temple.[34]

The highly significant act of the water-libation had to be performed by the priest in such a way that all the surrounding people were able to see that he did in fact pour the water into the bowl on the altar. Once it happened that a priest of the Baitos family, of the Sadducees, who were in principle opposed to the ceremony of water-libation, poured the water on to his feet, whereupon the crowd pelted him with their ethrogs. From that time onward it became customary for the priest to be admonished before performing the libation with the words, " Lift up your hand! " so that everybody could see that the jet of water issuing forth from the golden pitcher descended to its proper place, the western bowl on top of the altar.[35]

By the time the water-libation was finished the eastern side of the sky began to lighten. The time to offer the daily morning sacrifice was at hand, and so a new day of feasting and rejoicing began.

III

In order to make this complex ritual clear we need first of all to give its main component features as simple headings. The daily routine of the ritual comprised the following acts :

1 The covering of the altar with green willow branches
2 The circumambulation of the altar with the lulabs
3 The beating of the altar with palm branches or willow branches
4 The lighting of the lamps
5 The torch dance
6 Songs accompanied by numerous musical instruments ; repeated blasts of trumpets
7 The procession to the Siloam beginning at cock-crow
8 The water-drawing and the libation on the altar
9 The libation of wine

In addition to these, two further points should be mentioned, though not belonging to the daily ritual of the Temple. These two points, the significance of which will be discussed later, are :

10 The tumult with the lulabs on the Sabbath, and
11 The " lightheadedness," which led to the building of special galleries for the women

It would be easy to show that many of these points coincide with the elements of the New Year ritual, the centre and the climax of all the religious activities of the year,[36] as performed in Egypt, Babylonia and Canaan. The purpose of these central rituals was to reinvigorate nature for the duration of the new year just opening. Mythical elements, which were inseparably interwoven with the ritual, professed to supply the alleged reasons for the performance of the various ritual acts. The ritual was pronounced by these myths to be a re-enactment of the traditional creation of the world. That is, in the ritual itself the myth was declared to be the primary element and the ritual the secondary. Modern research has brought forth reasons for reversing this order, and for regarding the ritual as the primary element, in relation to which the myth is but secondary. This is the view held by Hooke, Hocart and others, who contend that the myth is but a secondary interpretation of the ritual, while actually the ritual is performed with an immediate practical purpose in view. Of the mythical associations of the water-libation in the Second Temple we shall hear later ; at this point we must discuss the immediate purpose of the ritual itself.

Even had I not mentioned already that the festivities were performed at the time of the year in which the beginning of the rainfall should occur, it would become sufficiently clear from the list of eleven points enumerated above, that the purpose of the ceremonies could be none other than one, namely, to induce the fall of rain. Each and every one of these eleven elements has indeed numerous parallels in the rain-making ceremonies of many other peoples, examples of which abound in *The Golden Bough* of Frazer and in other collections and studies. These parallels may help to establish the hidden meaning of the ceremonies of the "Joy of the House of Water-Drawing," a meaning that in the days of their actual performance was already mostly forgotten. We may establish that the altar covered with green branches stands for the earth itself; that circumambulations have been and still are performed by many peoples in their rain-making ceremonies. The lighting of the tall candelabra, as the lighting of new fire in general, would indicate new life beginning with the new year,[37] while the fourfold arrangement of the lamps, as well as the four ladders, four priestly youths, the shaking of the lulab towards the four cardinal points, would show the connection between the feast and the four winds, as also in other places ritual acts of a fourfold arrangement had an inner connection with the four points of the earth.[38] The ritual-mythical conception of lightning as torches in the Gilgamesh-Epic,[39] in the legend of Salmoneus, king of Elis,[40] and elsewhere, as well as the occurrence of torch-dances in ancient Mesopotamian and Canaanite rituals,[41] and the display of fire in the rain-making ceremonies of many other peoples[42]—all these would indicate that the Jerusalem torch-dances, too, were originally intended to bring about lightning, which is an accompanying phenomenon of stormy, hence abundant, rains. But even without turning elsewhere for explanation, the true purport of the torch-dances is elucidated by a Jewish legend according to which Hiram, king of Tyre, tried by similar artificial means to imitate lightning.[43] Of the prostrations, jumps and dances, which were also performed without torches,[44] it need only be remarked in short that among quite a number of other peoples, both European, Oriental and primitive, the practice is well known of performing high leaps in order to ensure the growth of the crops to an equal height.[45] The singing and playing on musical instruments and the other sound effects are methods resorted to, whenever rain is needed, by a great number of peoples, among them various Arab and Oriental Jewish communities.[46] The same purpose was served also by the repeated blasts, which when produced by the shofar-horn were also regarded by the ancient Jews themselves as the surest means of producing rain in times of drought.[47]

It seems superfluous to point out that the festive procession to the Siloam, the drawing of the water and its subsequent pouring out into the western bowl on the altar (the west is the only side from which the rain clouds come in Palestine) is a simple and straightforward rain-making ceremony. Processions, water-drawings and libations are in fact the most widespread elements of the whole rain-making complex. To mention only one example : the inhabitants of *Kafr Silwān* (that is, the village of Siloam), the Arab village next to Jerusalem, go down in procession in times of drought to the same well of Siloam out of which the water was drawn for the libation of the second Temple.[48] It will, perhaps, be of more interest to show that the cockcrow, at the sound of which the festive procession began, was no mere time-signal but the revelation of the propitious hour in which the success of the performance was most probable. The cock was regarded by the Jews, as well as by other peoples, as a bird of presage having special influence on the weather.[49] An important but hitherto insufficiently explained role was played by a sacred cock in the water-drawing, carrying and pouring ritual at Hierapolis in Syria, which contains quite a number of highly suggestive parallels to the Jerusalem ceremony.[50] It is Lucian who tells us in his famous *De dea Syria* that a great sacred assembly used to be held twice a year on the banks of the Euphrates. The people filled vessels with the water of the river, sealed them with wax, and presented them to a certain holy cock which dwelled hard by the lake. This bird on receiving the vessels from the bearers inspected the seals and pecked away the wax, receiving for this ritually significant action a remuneration in money. After this the bearers carried the water to the Temple and poured it into the mouth of a chasm that lay there beneath the Temple.[51] But more than that. A genuine talmudic tradition tells of a pagan temple where in days of drought a cock used to be sacrificed, whereupon rain fell.[52] So much for the cock.

As to the sacrificial use of wine, Robertson Smith

has remarked that it " seems to have been well-nigh universal wherever the grape was known ";[53] moreover, the libation of wine and other alcoholic beverages in rain-making ceremonies was habitual among quite a number of peoples.[54]

As to the tumult that took place on the Sabbath at the distribution of the lulabs, particulars told of it permit us to conclude that the fight was not an occasional outburst brought about by the high spirits of the celebrating crowd—such as, for example, the pelting of the Sadducee priest with the ethrogs[55]—but a regular traditional, if not ritual, institution. The Mishnah records that on the Friday the elders laid their lulabs in a special chamber, apart from those of the general public, in order to avoid being jostled on the Sabbath by the crowd.[56] Hence it appears that the tumultuous scene was expected each year. This would be quite in keeping with the rite of beating the altar with palm or willow branches, which was performed on the seventh day of the feast. The beating of the altar was followed by the throwing away of the lulabs by the children, a proceeding that was also probably of a tumultuous nature. As to the ritual significance of beating with green branches, this served elsewhere either to ensure the fall of rain and through it the fertility of the earth, or, like the " Lebensrute " of Germanic peoples and the Lupercal leather-straps in ancient Rome, to give fertility to human beings.[57] The belief that beatings promote the growth of plants is implicit in the following saying of Rabbi Simon:

There is no single grass which has not its *mazal* [guardian angel] in the firmament, which beats it and says to it: grow![58]

And at least one example is known of primitive horticulturists who actually beat their plants to make them grow.[59] Also the belief in the beneficial effect on human beings of willow branches in particular is attested in talmudic literature. The Jerusalem Talmud records that willow-branches were waved over sick persons as a remedy.[60] We may note in this connection that in the Jewish community of Tripoli, North Africa, the supplicants, gathered in the synagogue on the seventh day of the Feast of Tabernacles, used to beat one another with willow branches.[61]

According to rabbinic sources the lulab was regarded as a powerful weapon against Satan[62] as well as a symbol of a spiritual victory won by Israel over the Gentiles in the contest of the danger-fraught days of the New Year, when the fate of every people is being decided before the heavenly justice. The appearance of Israel with the triumphal palm branches in their hands shows that they have come out victorious.

The lulab is as one who takes, conquers and comes. As usual in the world, when two competing racers have run a race, the one who is taken by the Eparch (the Prefect) on his right side is the winner. So at New Year all pass by before God like the Sons of Meron and nobody knows who has won, whether Israel or the Nations of the World. . . . But as soon as the first day of *Sukkoth* (the Feast of Tabernacles) arrives and all Israel, old and young, go out with their lulabs in their hands, everybody knows that Israel has won in the court, and all their sins are forgiven, and they know that they have won. . . . Verily, you are brought the good tiding that you have conquered the Nations of the World. . . .[63]

In another passage the contest is compared to a trial before a law-court:

A parable : two entered to the judge and we do not know whom he has made winner. But when we see the one carrying a palm branch in his hand we know that he has won. So Israel and the Rulers of the Nations enter the Court before the Holy One blessed be He on New Year, and we do not know who shall win. But when Israel come out from before the Holy One blessed be He and their lulabs are in their hands and their ethrogs are in their hands, we know that Israel are the winners.[64]

The spiritual victory of Israel over the nations is spoken of in this passage as the winning of a case in the law-courts. This is in conformity with earlier Hebrew thought, in which—as Pedersen pointed out —the victory over enemies is " not different from victory in judicial proceedings."[65] The same concept goes back to even more ancient times in the Near East. In the myth of Horus at Edfu the victory of Horus over his enemies is described as his " justification " before the tribunal of the gods in the " Broad Hall."[66]

The ritual combat itself is not only a well-attested element in the New Year ritual of ancient Near Eastern peoples,[67] but finds a place in the ritual of a much wider circle of peoples.[68] The ritual combat is, to put it briefly, an organic part of the life-giving ritual. The beneficent forces of nature which must start afresh with the opening New Year cannot do so until the opposing forces of evil have been subdued. The forces of evil which appear in various forms are identified with the primordial forces of chaos which were originally opposed to the act of creation but were overcome by the creator. The ritual combat is thus at the same time also the commemorative representation of that first and greatest combat between the creative forces of the Good and the opposing, obstructing Evil.

The possibility of yet another and more immediate purpose of the ritual combat should not be left unmentioned in this connection. In Morocco, as well as in other places, all kinds of games of ball and tug-of-war are resorted to in rain-making ceremonies. Westermarck inferred from the data collected by himself and by others in North Africa that the essential function of such games as a weather-charm is to bring about a change in the weather through the movements and changing fortunes of the games.[69] Ceremonial combats for the purpose of producing rain seem to have occurred also among the ancient Lybians and the inhabitants of Caesarea (the so-called " Caterva ").[70]

We have last to touch upon the subject of the " lightheadedness " of the people, to suppress which the sages had to make repeated " amendments " until they finally settled the matter by relegating the women to special galleries. This " lightheadedness " was not, as may appear at first sight, a spontaneous expression of the festive gaiety. To rejoice was a biblical command also on many other festive occasions that drew large crowds to the Temple,[71] and it is hard to understand why self-control should be so specially relaxed precisely on this of all feasts, unless there was a particular reason for it. In the next chapter we shall try to throw some light on the mythological and conceptual background against which we have to view this, presumably ritual, lightheadedness.

IV

Let us now refer briefly to the important inner evidence consisting of numerous sayings and proverbs of talmudic sages confirming the conclusions reached above by anthropological methods. The heads of the two competing schools, Rabbi Yishmael and Rabbi Akiba, who lived some decades after the destruction of the Second Temple (first and second centuries C.E.), both agreed that the Feast of Tabernacles is the time when the amount of rain for the following year is being decided upon in heaven. Rabbi Akiba moreover said :

> The Torah (the Law, referring to the Pentateuch) said, Pour out water at the Feast (of the Water-libation) which is the period of rains, that the rains may be blessed for you.[72]

Again, Rabbi Eliezer said:

> When on the Feast of Tabernacles the water-libations are carried out, Deep says to Deep, Let thy waters spring forth, I hear the voice of two friends (namely, the water and the wine poured on to the altar).[73]

The true significance of this saying will become clear in the next chapter. Thus at least concerning the purpose and working of the central feature of the ritual, namely, the water-libation, our explanation is fully corroborated by sages, some of whom may have personally witnessed in their early days that grandest of all Jewish festivals.

Another problem to which the sages of the Talmud applied themselves with interest concerns the origin of the ritual of water-libation. The prevalent opinion was that the water-libation was a command of the Torah, and as no overt mention of it is to be found in the Pentateuch, some sages, such as Rabbi Akiba and Rabbi Jehuda ben B'thera, strove to read into certain passages of the Bible dealing with the Feast of Tabernacles,[74] the word *mayim*, water, which they then took for an enigmatic instruction to perform the libation of the water.[75] Other sages simply stated that the water-libation and the use of the willow branches were instituted by Moses, and already existed as a Mosaic tradition in the days of the First Temple.[76] According to talmudic legend the ritual of water-libation on the Feast of Tabernacles was performed even in days preceding the building of the Temple by Solomon. King David performed the ritual libation, to fetch the water for which three of his "mighty men" willingly risked their lives.[77] Other legends have it that the prototype of the libation of water and wine on the Feast of Tabernacles was the libation of these two liquids performed by Jacob over the stone of Bethel on which he slept and dreamt his famous dream.[78]

Now, apart from legends, the fact is that nowhere in the Bible is there any mention made of any connection between the Feast of Tabernacles and a ritual libation of water. On the other hand, several libations are recorded in the Bible as a means of bringing about the fall of rain, though the connection between the libation and the ensuing rain is in no instance as clear as with the water-libation in the Second Temple. Samuel having gathered the people together at Mizpeh, they " drew water and poured it out before the Lord and fasted." Samuel then offered a lamb unto the Lord and cried unto Him, and the Lord heard him and " thundered with a great thunder on that day."[79] Another time, in the days of harvest, that is in the middle of the rainless Palestinian summer, Samuel only called to the Lord without accompanying his call with a water-libation, and God sent thunder and rain upon the awe-struck people.[80]

At a later age, a regular rain-making competition took place between Elijah and the prophets of Baal on Mount Carmel.[81] In this competition both Elijah and the prophets of Baal performed a number of ritual acts, some of which were common to both, while some were peculiar to either party. We cannot here enter in detail into these rituals, which would necessitate a special study.[82] But let us place the two sets of ritual elements side by side for a comparison:

The Baal-prophets	Elijah
1 Built an altar	1 Built an altar
2 Slaughtered a bullock and	2 Slaughtered a bullock and
3 placed it on the wood on the altar without setting the wood on fire	3 placed it on the wood on the altar without setting the wood on fire
4 Called on the name of Baal : " O Baal hear us ! "	4 Called on the name of God : " Hear me, O Lord ! "
5 Leapt around the altar	5 Made a trench around the altar and filled it with water
6 Cut themselves with knives and lancets till the blood gushed out upon them	

Thus the main difference between the rainmaking procedure of the Baal-prophets and that of Elijah was, apart from each calling his own god, that the prophets of Baal tried to produce rain by leaping about their altar and shedding their own blood, while Elijah had a trench made around the altar and had water poured on to the altar until the water filled the trench. Now, as to the procedure of Elijah, it evidently was a precursor of the later Jewish water-libation. But at least one of the rites peculiar to the Baal-prophets may too have succeeded in penetrating into the Jewish ritual, namely, the leaping around the altar, which in the Second Temple ritual appears as a mere circumambulation of the altar. However that may be, the leaping itself has survived among the Arabs of Palestine in its original form as a rite of leaping with bended knees, this ritual dance, now called *dabke*, being performed in order to produce rain.[83]

As to the other rite performed only by the Baal-prophets, the cutting themselves with knives or lancets, we would not connect it with the injuries that the celebrating people inflicted upon one another on the Sabbath-tumult. It is, however, interesting to note that the ritual combat sometimes does take an emphatically bloody character, as, for instance, in Abyssinia, where the ceremonial fights between the villages for obtaining rain retained their cruelty and bloodshed in spite of the attempted reform of the emperor Menelik.[84] Self-laceration is practised as a rain-charm by several primitive peoples,[85] while oriental Jewish communities content themselves with substituting the blood of slaughtered animals for the human blood. To name only one instance, the Jews of Kurdistan in their rain-charms smear the blood of slaughtered animals upon their foreheads.[86]

V

To complete the picture before leaving this topic, we think it should not be left unmentioned that according to biblical evidence prayers for rain among the ancient Hebrews were coeval with rain-charms. Of Samuel we have just heard that apart from performing a ritual he also cried unto the Lord for rain.[87] The rain-making of Elijah, as well as that of the Baal-prophets, was accompanied by calling upon the Deity.[88] In later times the rain-making ceremony vanished altogether—to return only at the close of the Second Temple period—and only the prayer remained. Of King Solomon it is stated that he said in his prayer at the dedication of the Temple:

> When heaven is shut up and there is no rain . . . if they pray toward this place . . . then hear thou in heaven. . . .[89]

In the days of the prophet Joel, when there was a heavy drought, the prophet admonished his people :

> Sanctify ye a fast, call a solemn assembly . . . and cry unto the Lord.[90]

Again Judea suffered from dearth, in the days of Jeremiah, but God warned the prophet not to pray for the people[91]: from this it is evident that prayers were the usual means of averting drought in the times of Jeremiah. These occasional prayers for rain which were offered up in times of need finally became settled, after the erection of the Second Temple, as a regular ritual institution connected with the Feast of Tabernacles. Thus according to the evidence of the Prophet Zechariah:

> . . . every one that is left of all the nations which came against Jerusalem shall even go up from year to year to worship the King, the Lord of hosts, and to keep the feast of tabernacles. And it shall be, that whoso will not come up of all the families of the earth unto Jerusalem to worship the King the Lord of hosts, even upon them shall be no rain. . . .[92]

Beneath the obvious religious content of these words, one cannot fail to discern the first faint indications of a conception, so prevalent in later Judaism, of the Temple as the centre of blessing, on which depended the well-being not only of the people of Israel but also of all the nations of the world.

This concept, which is closely interwoven with a number of myths on the cosmic significance and connections of the Temple, will constitute the theme of our next chapter.

1 As to the versions of the name of the festival cf. Venetianer, *Die Eleusinischen Mysterien im Tempel zu Jerusalem*, in Brüll's *Populär-wissenschaftliche Monatsblätter*, xvii, reprint, Frankfurt a. M., 1897, pp. 3 sqq.; Joseph Hochmann, *Jerusalem Temple Festivities*, London, n.d., pp. 54 sqq.; D. Feuchtwang, *Das Wasseropfer und die damit verbundenen Zeremonien*, *Monatschrift für die Geschichte und Wissenschaft des Judentums*, vols. liv–lv, reprint, Wien, 1911, p. 41; M. Stein, in *Tarbiz* (in Hebrew), Jerusalem, vol. i, pp. 135 sq.; S. Liebermann, in *Qiryath Sepher* (in Hebrew), Jerusalem, vol. xii, p. 56; Patai, *The Control of Rain in Ancient Palestine*, in *Hebrew Union College Annual*, Cincinnati, vol. xiv, p. 259; id., *Man and Earth in Hebrew Custom, Belief and Legend* (in Hebrew), vol. ii, Jerusalem, 1943, p. 161.

2 On the Feast of Tabernacles (Sukkoth) cf. Grunwald, *Vorgeschichte des Sukkothrituals*, in *Jahrbuch für Jüdische Volkskunde*, vol. i, Berlin-Wien, 1923, pp. 427 sqq.; I. Elbogen, *Die Feier der drei Wallfahrtsfeste im zweiten Tempel*, 46. *Bericht der Hochschule* für die Wissenschaft des Judentums, Berlin, 1929.

3 According to the Hebrew calendar from the 15th to the 22nd of the month Tishri, the first of which is the New Year.

4 M. Tamid 3, 2.

5 Ex. 29, 39; Num. 28, 4; B. Pes. 58a sq.; Tos. Suk. 4, 5, p. 198; B. Suk. 53a; Y. Suk. 55b mid.

6 B. Yoma 26b; Tos. Suk. 3, 16, p. 197; sometimes the water-libation was performed before the daily morning-offering, even at night-time, cf. Y. Suk. 54d top.

7 B. Suk. 53a; Y. Suk. 55b mid.

8 Y. Suk. 54b bot. The Arabic village on the same spot is

called now *Kalonia*, while the Jewish village built on the hill near by is called by the ancient Hebrew name, *Motza*.

9 M. Suk. 4, 5; B. Suk. 45a–b and Rashi ib.

10 M. Suk. 4, 5; B. Suk. 38b.

11 So according to the text of the Mishnah Suk. 4, 6 of the Jerusalem Talmud, Suk. 54b top. The Mishnah text of the Babylonian Talmud, Suk. 45a, as well as the separate editions of the Mishnah, have "beat them on the ground at the sides of the altar."

12 M. Suk. 4, 6–7; Tos. Suk. 2, 10, p. 195; Y. Suk. 54a mid., b bot.; B. Suk. 41b, 43a–b, 44a, 46b.

13 B. Suk. 47b–48a.

14 M. Suk. 4, 4 and Obadia di Bertinoro ib.

15 M. Suk. 5, 1.

16 M. Suk. 5, 2; Tos. Suk. 4, 1; M. Mid. 2, 5; Y. Suk. 55b mid.; B. Suk. 52a.

17 According to B. Suk. 52b the lamps were 50 cubits high, according to Y. Suk. 55b mid.—100 cubits. One cubit corresponds to 17.6 inches or about 44 cms.

18 M. Suk. 5, 2; B. Suk. 52b.

19 Y. Suk. 55b bot.

20 M. Suk. 5, 2; B. Suk. 53a; Y. Suk. 55b top.

21 M. Suk. 5, 4; Tos. Suk. 4, 2, p. 198.

22 Tos. Suk. 4, 4, p. 198; Y. Suk. 55b bot.–c top; B. Suk. 53a.

23 Y. Suk. 55b–c; Targum Sheni ad Esth. 3, 8; M. Suk. 5, 4; Tos. Suk. 4, 2–3, p. 198; B. Suk. 53a.

24 M. Suk. 5, 4; Tos. Suk. 4, 7, p. 198 sq.

25 Psalms 120–134; M. Suk. 4, 4; M. Mid. 2, 5; Tos. Suk. 4, 7–9, p. 198 sq.

26 According to sep. edd. of the Mishnah Suk. 4, 4.

27 M. Suk. 5, 4; Tos. Suk. 4, 10, p. 199

28 On this gate cf. J. Morgenstern, *The Gates of Righteousness*, in *Hebrew Union College Annual*, Cincinnati, vol. vi, pp. 1 sqq.

29 The reference is to Eze. 8, 16.

30 M. Suk. 5, 4; on the sun-cult in the Temple of Jerusalem cf. Hollis, in Hooke, *Myth and Ritual*, Oxford, 1933,

pp. 87 sqq.; cf. Frazer, *The Worship of Nature*, vol. I, London, 1926, pp. 553 sqq. On the historical background of this saying cf. J. Morgenstern, *op. cit.* pp. 31 sqq.

31 Accordingly we have to suppose that only the inner surface of the bowls was visible. They may have been sunk into the surface of the altar. Cf. the so-called "cup-marks" on many an ancient stone altar in Palestine and Transjordan.

32 According to another version traditioned by Rabbi Jehuda, the libation consisted only of one "log," i.e. about half a litre, but was performed also on the eighth day of the feast, cf. M. Suk. 4, 9.

33 Cf. B. Suk. 49a: "Rabbi Eleazar ben Zadok stated, there was a small passage-way between the ascent and the altar." The ascent, or ramp, did not adjoin closely to the altar at the top, but was removed from it by two cubits. This small space was fenced up along its four sides, thus forming a vat which reached down to the marble floor of the court. Cf. Rashi *ad loc.*

34 M. Suk. 4, 9.; Tos. Suk. 3, 14–15, p. 197; Tos. Me'ila 1, 16, p. 558; Y. Suk. 54c bot., d top; B. Suk. 48b, 49a–b.

35 M. Suk. 4, 9; Tos. Suk. 3, 16, p. 197; Y. Suk. 54d mid.; B. Suk. 48b; B. Yoma 26b; B. Pes. 57a; Josephus Flavius, *Antiquities*, xiii, 13, 5.

36 Hooke, *Myth and Ritual*, p. 8.

37 Frazer, *The Golden Bough*, 3rd ed., vol. i, pp. 251, 303; vol. x, p. 138.

38 Mannhardt, *Antike Wald- und Feldkulte*, 2nd ed., Berlin, 1905, p. 263, n. 1; Frazer, *op. cit.* iii, 154; Hocart, *Kings and Councillors*, Cairo, 1936, p. 253.

39 Gilgamesh-epic, Table xi, lines 98–116.

40 Apollodorus, i, 9, 7; cf. J. Harrison, *Themis*, Cambridge, 1912, pp. 79 sq.

41 Hooke, *The Origins of Early Semitic Ritual*, London, 1938, pp. 53 sq.

42 H. Pfannenschmied, *Das Weihwasser im heidnischen und*

christlichen Kultus, Hannover, 1869, p. 79 ; Mannhardt, *Wald- und Feldkulte*, i. *Der Baumkultus der Germanen*, 2nd ed., Berlin, 1904, pp. 506, 511, 534 sq. ; Goldziher, *Muhammedanische Studien*, vol. i, Halle, 1888, pp. 34 sq. ; Frazer, *op. cit.* i, 248, 251, 300, 303 ; vii, 38, 54, 55, 59 ; Patai, *The Control of Rain*, p. 274 ; id. *Man and Earth*, ii, 175 sqq.

43 'Inyan Hiram Melekh Tzor, in Jellinek, *Beth Hamidrash*, vol. v, p. 111 ; Yalqut Shime'oni ii. § 367 ad Eze. 28 ; cf. also Ginzberg, *The Legends of the Jews*, vol. vi, pp. 424 sq.

44 Y. Suk. 55b–c.

45 Oesterley, *The Sacred Dance*, Cambridge, 1923, pp. 149 sqq. ; Frazer, *op. cit.* i, 137 sq. ; vii, 95, 111 sq., 186 sq. ; ix, 231 sq. ; Patai, *Man and Earth*, ii, 151 sqq., 177 sq.

46 J. Harrison, *Themis*, 77 sq. ; Kahle, *Palästina-Jahrbuch*, vol. viii, 1912, p. 162 ; Westermarck, *Ceremonies and Beliefs Connected with Agriculture, etc., in Morocco*, Helsingfors, 1913, pp. 109, 123 ; Brauer, *Ethnologie der jemenitischen Juden*, Heidelberg, 1934, p. 213 ; Meyouhas, *Ma'asiyyoth 'am libhne qedem*, Jerusalem, 1938, p. 165 ; Frazer, *op. cit.* i, 250, 255, 261, 267 sq., 276, 284, 287, 293 sq.

47 M. Ta'an, 1, 6 ; 3, 1–2 ; cf. Patai, *The Control of Rain*, 280 sq.

48 *Zeitschrift für alttestamentliche Wissenschaft*, 1900, pp. 111 sq. ; Kahle, *Palästina-Jahrbuch*, vol. vi, p. 94 ; Patai, *Hamayim* (in Hebrew), Tel-Aviv, 1936, p. 52.

49 Cf. Patai, *The Control of Rain*, pp. 269 sqq.

50 Cf. *Revue des études Juives*, vol. xxxvi, p. 317 ; vol. xliii, p. 195 ; Lagrange, *Études sur les religions Semitiques*, 2nd ed., Paris, 1905, pp. 166 sq. ; Rieger, *Jewish Quarterly Review*, 1926, January, p. 232. On the cock in rain-charms cf. also Gressmann, *Marti-Festschrift*, pp. 88 sqq. ; Jaussen, *Revue Biblique*, xxxiii, 574 sqq.

51 Lucian, *de dea Syria*, 13 and 48, ed. Strong and Garstang, pp. 51 sq. As to " the sea "=the Euphrates, cf. Philo-

stratus, *Vita Apoll.* i, 20 ; Robertson Smith, *Engl. Hist. Rev.* (1887), p. 312 ; id., *The Religion of the Semites*, 3rd ed., p. 232. Some scholars, among them Strong and Garstang, ib., contend that the cock referred to by Lucian was a priest who for one reason or another was called by this name. Against them Clemen maintains that the reference is to a real cock. Cf. Carl Clemen, *Lukians Schrift über die syrische Göttin*, Der Alte Orient, Leipzig, 1938, vol. xxxvii, 3-4, p. 51. On the cock of Hierapolis cf. also Gressmann, *Der heilige Hahn zu Hierapolis in Syrien*, Beihefte zur Zeitschrift für die alttestamentliche Wissenschaft, xli, 1925, p. 88.

52 B. ʿAb. Zara 55a. The Aramaic word "gabhra" used in this connection to denote cock is by some scholars understood in its original sense as "man," f. i. Cook, in Robertson Smith, *op. cit.* p. 581, n. 5.

53 Robertson Smith, *op. cit.* p. 220 ; cf. the note of Cook ib. pp. 574 sqq.

54 Cf. Frazer, *op. cit.* i, 250 ; ii, 367, 370.

55 M. Suk. 4, 9. Cf. Josephus, *Ant.* xiii, 13, 5.

56 Cf. the explanation of Obadia di Bertinoro *ad loc.*

57 Hartland, *The Legend of Perseus*, London, 1894–96, vol. i, p. 171 ; id., *Primitive Paternity*, London, 1909, vol. i, pp. 100, 108 ; Preller, *Römische Mythologie*, 3rd ed., Berlin, 1881–83, vol. i, p. 389; A. de Gubernatis, *Die Thiere in der indogerm. Myth.*, 173 sq.; Mannhardt, *Wald und Feldkulte* i, 251 sq.; Ovid, *Fasti*, ii, 425, and Frazer, *The Fasti of Ovid*, London, 1929, vol. ii, p. 331, 383; id., *The Golden Bough*, ix, 362 ; Ploss-Bartels-Reitzenstein, *Das Weib*, 11th ed., Berlin, 1927, vol. ii, p. 315.

58 Gen. Rab. 10, 6, p. 79 ; cf. the Slavonic Book of Henoch, 19, 4 ; the same idea with some elaboration in Zohar Gen. (Hashmatoth), p. 251a of the Wilna ed.

59 In New Caledonia, cf. Frazer, *The Golden Bough*, ix, 264.

60 Y. Suk. 54a mid.

61 Benyamin, Yisrael ben Yosef, *Sepher massaʿe Yisrael*, Lyck, 1859, p. 127. English translation (*Eight Years in Asia and Africa*, Hanover, 1863, p. 331).

62 B. Suk. 38a ; B. Menahoth 62a.
63 Midrash Shoher Tobh, Ps. 17.
64 Yalqut Shime'oni, § 651 ; cf. Lev. Rab. 30, 2.
65 Pedersen, *Israel*, i–ii (1926), p. 539 (note to p. 429), referring to the following passages : 1 Sam. 14, 47; Ex. 22, 8; Deut. 25, 1; 1 Kings 8, 32; Ps. 37, 33; Prov. 12, 2; 17, 15; Job 40, 8; Isa. 29, 21; 54, 17.
66 A.M. Blackman and H. W. Fairman, "The Myth of Horus at Edfu II," *The Journal of Egyptian Archaeology*, vol. xxviii. (London, 1942), p. 32.
67 Hooke, *Myth and Ritual*, 8, 24, 32, 84, 163; Blackman and Fairman, *op. cit.* pp. 32 sqq.; Ivan Engnell, *Studies in Divine Kingship in the Ancient Near East,* Uppsala, 1943, p. 36.
68 Cf. Hocart, *Kings and Councillors*, Cairo, 1936, *pass.*
69 Westermarck, *Ritual and Belief in Morocco*, London, 1926, vol. ii, p. 271; cf. Frazer, *The Golden Bough*, ix, 179 sq.
70 Westermarck, *op. cit.*, ii, 272, quoting St. Augustine, *De doctr. Christ.*, IV, 24 (53).
71 Lev. 28, 40 ; Deut. 12, 7, 11–12, 17–18 ; 14, 26 ; 16, 11, 14 ; 26, 11 ; 27, 7 ; cf. Neh. 8, 12–17.
72 Tos. Suk. 3, 18, p. 197 sq.; cf. Tos. Rosh Hash. 1, 12, 13, p. 210 ; Y. Rosh Hash. 57b mid.; B. Rosh Hash. 16a ; also M. Rosh Hash. 1, 2 ; B. Ta'an. 2a–b; Y. Suk. 54b mid.; Y. Shebi'it 33b bot. ; Pesiqta di Rabh Kahana, ed. Buber, 193b.
73 B. Ta'an. 25b and Rashi *ad loc.*
74 Num. 29, 19, 31, 33.
75 Y. Rosh Hash. 57b mid. ; cf. Y. Suk. 54b mid. ; B. Ta'an. 2b bot.; Y. Shebi'it 33b bot.; Pesiqta di Rabh Kahana, ed. Buber, 193b.
76 Y. Suk. 54b mid. ; cf. Y. Shebi'it 33b mid. and bot.; Y. Rosh Hash. 57b mid.; B. Suk. 34a, 44a sq.; B. Ta'an. 3a.
77 Y. Sanh. 20c top. Cf. Ruth Rab. 2, 9 end. The reference is to 2 Sam. 23, 15–17.
78 Gen. Rab. 78, 16, p. 936 ; Targum Yer. ad Gen. 35, 14. Cf. Book of Jub. 31, 3 ; 32, 4 sqq.

79 1 Sam. 7, 3–10.
80 1 Sam. 12, 17–18.
81 1 Kings 18.
82 Cf. Patai, *Man and Earth*, ii, 145 sqq.; id., *The Control of Rain*, pp. 254 sqq.
83 Dalman, *Arbeit und Sitte in Palästina*, vol. i, Gütersloh, 1928, p. 146 ; id. *Palästinensischer Diwan*, Leipzig, 1901, pp. 267 sqq., 273. Cf. also the ancient Arab rite of the circumambulation of the Holy Stone (the *Ka'aba*) in Mecca in rain-making ceremonies, Wellhausen, *Reste arabischen Heidentums*, Berlin, 1897, p. 141. Cf. also Cook, in Robertson Smith, *The Religion of the Semites*, 3rd ed., p. 671 sq.
84 Frazer, *The Golden Bough*, i, 256 sqq.
85 *Op. cit.*, pp. 257 sqq.
86 Brauer, in *Magnes Anniversary Book* (in Hebrew), Jerusalem, 1938, p. 53.
87 1 Sam. 7, 5, 9; 12, 17–18.
88 1 Kings 18, 24, 26, 28, 36–37.
89 1 Kings 8, 35–36.
90 Joel 1, 14.
91 Jer. 14, 11.
92 Zech. 14, 17–18; cf. also 10, 1.

Chapter Three

TEMPLE AND CREATION MYTHS

In the previous chapter it has been shown that the immediate purpose of the great festivity called "The Joy of the House of Water-Drawing," performed in the Second Temple of Jerusalem, was to ensure the fall of rain. In this chapter we shall inquire into the mythical connotations of this great feast.

Our contention was that the Joy of the House of Water-Drawing was a New Year ritual of the type performed year after year in numerous cult-centres of the ancient East. Accordingly we should expect the mythical connotations of the feast to have to do mainly with the traditional creation of the world. And, indeed, we shall not be disappointed in this expectation.

I

First it is needful to recall a detail of the festive ritual which we have so far not discussed. This is the singing of the fifteen Songs of Ascents by the Levites as they stood on the fifteen steps leading from the "Women's Court" up to the inner "Court of the Israelites."[1] These fifteen short Psalms (Ps. 120–134), each of which begins with the words *Shir hama'aloth*—"Song of Ascents,"[2] contain no express reference to the Feast of Tabernacles or to the ceremonies of the water-drawing and libation. But later sources, the same as those from which we drew the data for the description of the ritual, abound in legends referring to the mythical significance of these fifteen songs. These legends take us back directly into the mythical atmosphere of primeval cosmic events. They have, it is true, a historical setting, being connected with the person of King David ; nevertheless they are typical flood-legends, the like of which in other mythologies are closely bound up with creation-myths and are regarded by scholars as variations of the original theme of creation.

King David, so the legend runs, wished to build the Temple of the Lord upon pure, virgin soil. After he had bought the threshing floor of Arawna he began to dig into the earth in order to find out whether the place was virgin soil, undisturbed by human hands ever since the creation. When David reached the depth of fifteen hundred cubits he came upon a sherd, sure proof that man had once been present there. And David exclaimed :

" After all the trouble I have taken, now I find this sherd! " Whereupon God gave a voice to the sherd and it said : " This is not my original place, but when the earth was split asunder (at the giving of the Torah at Mount Sinai) I descended here. If you do not believe me—behold, *Tehom*, the Deep, lies beneath me!" David picked up the sherd and the waters of the Deep rose to engulf him. David said : " Whosoever knows a word that will put a stop to this Tehom, and does not say it, may he suffocate!" And Ahitophel,[3] who stood there, spoke the word and arrested the Deep.[4]

An older and fuller version of this legend is preserved in the Babylonian Talmud:

> Rabbi Johanan said . . . When David dug the Pits (that is, the perpendicular shafts reaching down under the Temple to the Deep), the Deep arose and threatened to submerge the world. "Is there anyone," inquired David, "who knows whether it is permitted to inscribe the [Ineffable] Name upon a sherd, and cast it into the Deep that its waves should subside?" There was none who answered a word. Said David, "Whoever knows the answer and does not speak, may he be suffocated!" Whereupon Ahitophel . . . said to him, "It is permitted." [David] thereupon inscribed the [Ineffable] Name upon a sherd, cast it into the Deep and it subsided sixteen thousand cubits. When he saw that it had subsided to such a great extent, he said, "The nearer it is to the (surface of the) earth, the better the earth can be kept watered," and he uttered the fifteen Songs of Ascents and the Deep reascended fifteen thousand cubits and remained one thousand cubits (below the surface).[5]

This legend, of which many other versions exist in traditional Jewish literature, has a remarkable parallel in a legend reported by Lucian in connection with the Temple of Hierapolis:

> But a further story is told by the men of Hierapolis, and a wonderful one it is; they say that in their country a mighty chasm appeared which received all the water (namely, of the deluge), and that Deukalion on this occurrence reared altars and founded a temple to Juno above this chasm. I have actually seen this chasm, it lies beneath the temple and is of very small dimensions. If it was once of large size, and was afterwards reduced to its present small dimensions, I know not: but the chasm which I saw is certainly very small. They maintain that their tale is proved by the following occurrence: twice in every year the water comes from the sea to the temple. This water is brought by the priests; but

besides them, all Syria and Arabia and many from beyond the Euphrates go down to the sea ; one and all bring its water which they first pour out in the temple ; then this water passes down into the chasm which, small though it be, holds a vast quantity of water.[6]

The points of contact between this legend and that of Jerusalem are too numerous to be mere coincidence. The Hierapolis legend speaks of the appearance of a chasm in which the waters of the deluge were swallowed up. The Jerusalem legend, though it records the digging of David, also speaks of something like a chasm which appeared when the earth trembled at the Revelation on Mount Sinai, so that the sherd fell into it. In another version of the Jerusalem legend the function of the sherd in keeping down the Deep is more pronounced. When David dug and found the sherd, he wanted to lift it.

The sherd said : "You cannot lift me." David said : "Why?" The sherd said: "Because I am here to press down the Deep." David asked : "And since when are you here ?" The sherd answered : "From the hour when God let His word be heard on Mount Sinai saying, 'I am the Lord thy God.'[7] At (that time) the earth trembled and sank, and I was put here to press down the Deep. . . .[8]

Still more explicit is the version that connects the temple-shafts directly with the creation of the world. According to this version, when

God created heaven and earth He also created the stone over the Deep, and engraved on it the Ineffable Name consisting of forty-two letters, and fixed the stone over the Deep in order to keep down its waters. . . . But when the generation of the deluge sinned, He removed the stone and immediately all the sources of the great Deep sprang up. And when David dug the shafts, the stone rolled aside and the waters came out and filled the whole world. . . . David took the stone and threw it back on the Deep whereupon the waters returned.[9]

Here it is expressly stated that the waters of the deluge issued from beneath the "stone," and that when David dug the shafts the Deep rose anew from beneath the "stone," and later again subsided beneath it. We shall later return to speak of this stone which was identified by legend with the so-called *Shetiyyah*-stone, the huge native rock upon which the Holy of Holies of the Jerusalem Temple was built.

The Hierapolis legend has it that the altars and the temple were built by Deukalion over the chasm after the waters of the deluge had subsided into it. In the Jerusalem legend, too, the building of the altar and the temple over the shaft follows the swallowing up of the waters in it, the altar being said to have been built by Noah, as reported in Genesis (8, 20). Late Jewish legends have it that Noah only rebuilt this altar, which had been already in use by Adam, Cain and Abel, and which was later to be used by Abraham, and finally included in the temple of Jerusalem.[10]

Thus the water-libations that were performed in both the Hierapolis and the Jerusalem temples are connected by the respective legends with the floods that were swallowed up in the chasms beneath the altars.

In Greece, too, one finds the idea that the waters of the deluge flowed down through a chasm. In Athens, within the great precinct overshadowed by the temple of Olympian Zeus, there was a smaller precinct of Olympian Earth, where a cleft, one cubit wide, was pointed out in the ground. Down that cleft the waters of the deluge were said to have disappeared, and down it were thrown every year cakes of wheaten meal kneaded with honey.[11] The name "Festival of Water-Bearing"[12] may be taken as an indication also that water was poured down the cleft.[13]

II

But to return to Jerusalem. The connection between the rain and the subterranean waters is often enough emphasized in rabbinic literature. It was a traditional belief that the fall of rain is matched by a corresponding rise of Tehom, the waters of the Deep. Rabbi Levi said:

> It is the way of the world, rain descends and Tehom rises.[14]

Rabbi Shimeon ben Eleazar said:

> There is no hand-breadth [of rain] that descends from above but has two hand-breadths [of water] raised towards it by the earth.[15]

We have already heard that the water-libation served not only to bring down the rain from heaven but also to raise the waters of the Deep. Rabbi Eliezer said:

> When on the Feast of Tabernacles the water-libations are carried out, Deep says unto Deep, Let thy waters spring forth, I hear the voice of two friends (namely, the water and the wine poured on to the altar).[16]

The raising of the waters of the deep, we now understand, was brought about also by the singing of the fifteen Songs of Ascents, which were said to have been sung for the first time by David for the same purpose.

It will be of interest to note that the concept of the correspondence between the falling of rain and the rising of the Deep may be traced back in northern Canaan to a period preceding that of the Talmud by some fifteen hundred years. In the Ras Shamra texts we read:

> There will be no dew, no showers,
> No surging up of the Deep.[17]

Another example of this idea comes from Assyria:

> On high Adad made scarce his rain,
> Beneath [the fountain] was stopped . . .[18]

Or, again, we have the complementary description:

> Adad let loose his showers, Ea opened his fountains . . .[19]

This is very much the same as the words of Genesis:

> The same day were all the fountains of the great Deep broken up, and the windows of heaven were opened.[20]

But to return to rabbinic material, in the name of Rabba an interesting mythological concept is reported following the saying of Rabbi Eliezer quoted earlier. Rabba said:

> I saw Ridya (the angel of rain) and he is like a three-year-old heifer with lips cleft asunder. He stood between the lower Deep and the upper Deep. He said to the upper Deep, Pour down your waters! and to the lower Deep he said, Let your waters spring up! . . .[21]

One would naturally be inclined to compare this water-bringing cosmic heifer to the heavenly cow of ancient Egypt,[22] sometimes identified with the sky-goddess Nut, who was usually depicted as the giver of rain.[23] The idea of symbolizing rain in the form of a bull seems to have been general in the ancient Near East. In the Ras Shamra texts, Baal, the god of storms and rains, was endowed with the strength of a bull, striking and destroying his enemies with his horns. When he was killed he was overcome in the form of a bull. He fell "like the bull under the sacrificer's knife." Aliyan Baal, the son of Baal, watches over the maintenance of springs and underground waters. The concept of the water as a fertilizing bull, or as an incentive for the cattle to mate, seems to underlie a passage in the Ras Shamra texts which describes a love scene between Aliyan Baal and a heifer.[24] With this should be compared the saying of Rabbi Jehuda ben Levi:

> In the hour when rain falls the cattle seeks [to fulfil] its task, that is, mates.[25]

Both in the Ras Shamra texts and, some one and a half millennia later, in the Jerusalem Temple legends, a scene in the yearly recurrent cycle of nature finds its poetic expression. The Ras Shamra texts depict the ceasing of the rain as the descent of Baal into the womb of the earth, which is followed later by the death of Aliyan Baal, that is, the disappearance or diminishing of springs and rivers.[26] There follow the dry and rainless months of the prolonged eastern summer characterized by the continuous sinking of the level of each still available source of water, such as the perennial streams, the few springs, and the cisterns in which the rain-water of the previous winter was stored up for drinking. After the first few rainy days in the autumn all this is suddenly changed. Opposite the rain falling from above, the waters from below actually seem to rise—and it is this situation, expected to come about in consequence of the water-libation, which is anticipated in the rabbinic legends.

The waters from above and the waters from below are in talmudic legends described as "the upper male waters" and "the lower female waters" respectively.[27] In the beginning, that is, before the Creation, "the world was but water in water."[28] Then God separated the two kinds of water from each other, relegating half of them to the firmament and half of them to the ocean.[29] This separation was not accomplished without resistance on the part of the waters. God said to them :

> "Divide yourselves into two halves, and let the one half mount upwards, and the second half (descend) below." And they disobeyed and mounted all of them upwards. Then the Holy One blessed be He said unto them : "I said, Let the half of you mount upwards, and instead all of you mounted upwards." Said the waters : We shall not descend! They were daring in the face of the Creator, and therefore were they called "daring waters."[30] What did the Holy One blessed be He? He stretched out his small finger and tore them into two parts, and one half of them fell down below against their will. . . .[31]

In other versions of this legend the traces of a primeval combat between God and the waters are even more pronounced:

The Holy One blessed be He stamped upon all the primeval waters and cast them into the Ocean. . . .[32]

. . . the waters rolled down and gathered into valleys . . . and at once the waters became haughty and rose to flood the earth as in the beginning, until the Holy One blessed be He scolded them and pressed them down beneath the soles of his feet. . . .[33]

Rabh Jehuda said in the name of Rabh: At the time when the Holy One blessed be He desired to create the world, he said to the angel of the sea: Open thy mouth and swallow all the waters of the world (that the dry land may be seen). He said unto him: Lord of the universe, it is enough that I remain with my own! Thereupon *He* struck him with his foot and killed him, as it is written, "He stirreth up the sea with his power and by his understanding he smiteth through Rahab."[34]

Many other versions also tell how God "kicked" the waters, "killed" them and pressed them together into the ocean.[35] It is also told in these legends that when the upper waters were forced to separate from the lower waters, they wept,[36] and so did the lower waters.[37] Ever since the separation of the heavenly waters from their earthly mates, they continuously long for reunion with them:

The only craving of the rains is for the earth. . . .[38]

The reason why God separated the upper waters from the lower waters is also given in the following version:

Why did the Holy One blessed be He separate them? Because the upper waters are male and the lower waters are female, and when they tried to unite they almost destroyed the world. In that hour the waters ascended the mountains and descended the valleys, the male waters were running after the female waters, until the Holy One blessed be He rebuked them, as it is written, "At thy rebuke they fled."[39]

In another highly suggestive version these lustful primeval elements are personified as the male and female Leviathan, the great sea-serpent :

Rabh Jehuda said in the name of Rabh : All that the Holy One blessed be He created in His world He created male and female. Likewise, Leviathan the fleeing serpent and Leviathan the crooked serpent He created male and female, and had they mated with one another they would have destroyed the world. What [then] did the Holy One blessed be He do ? He castrated the male and killed the female . . . as it is written, "And he will slay the dragon that is in the sea."[40]

The motif of separation and castration remind us, of course, of similar motifs contained in ancient Egyptian, Greek, Vedic, Chinese, Polynesian, American-Indian, African, and other creation myths,[41] while the portraiture of the cosmic sources of water as dragons is well known from the ancient Accadian, Canaanite and Israelite mythological imagery.[42] "Leviathan the fleeing serpent" of the Bible[43] appears already in the Ras Shamra poems as "Lotan the fleeing serpent," and also the "crooked serpent"[44] and the *tannin*, the primeval dragon[45] of the Bible, have their counterpart in the Ras Shamra texts.[46] Thus we arrive at the interesting fact that the mythical tales about the rebellion of the primeval waters which are to be found in rabbinic literature as late as the fifth century C.E. in quite a number of versions, contain motifs going back to ancient traditions attested in Canaanite culture already some two millennia earlier.

III

What was a mere threat in the days of creation came to pass later, in the days of the great flood. Thus we read in the Book of Henoch:

> And in those days shall punishment come from the Lord of Spirits, and He will open all the chambers of waters which are above the heavens, and of the fountains which are beneath the earth. And all the waters shall be joined with the waters: that which is above the heavens is the masculine, and the water which is beneath the earth is the feminine. And they shall destroy all who dwell on the earth and those who dwell under the ends of the heaven.[47]

Similarly also according to a late midrash:

> Rabbi Zadoq said: On the tenth of [the month of] Marheshwan all the creatures entered the Ark, and on the seventeenth of it there descended onto the earth the waters of the deluge which are male waters, and [waters] came up from the Deeps (*Tehomoth*) which are female waters, and they united and grew mighty to destroy the world. . . .[48]

The idea that floods and inundations are the result of a union between male and female waters goes back to age-old traditions in the ancient East. Side by side with the tradition of the destructive deluge as reported, for example, in the Gilgamesh-Epic (Table xi), there existed in ancient Mesopotamia other conceptions in which the beneficial inundations were clad in mythological imagery. The annual life-giving floods, caused by the rising of the waters of the Tigris and Euphrates, in consequence of which the dry fields were irrigated, were mythically represented as being the result of a union between male and female deities. In the introductory mythical section of a Sumerian incantation text, preserved on one of the early tablets from Nippur, the life-producing flood is pictured as being brought about by the union between two deities, Enki the god of the Deep, who had his dwelling in the Euphrates, and the goddess Ninella, a water deity, also referred to as Nintu, "the goddess of birth."[49] In this Sumerian text there is "expressed the symbolical parallel between the god pouring his 'water' into the 'ground' of the goddess and thus fructifying her, and the earth receiving water as a means of fertilization." The passage that speaks of a rainy season extending over nine months, "implies a parallel between the nine months of pregnancy and the process of fertilization until the fruit is ripe."[50] Also two other passages in Babylonian literature, concerning Enlil and Ninlil, and Ningirsu and Bau, "show that the water was regarded as the spermatozoa of the gods, and that the rise of the water in the two great rivers which irrigate that country was thought to be due to sexual union between a god and an earth goddess. . . ."[51] In this Babylonian conception the water is regarded as a male principle. That the same was true in Arabia is indicated by the fact that in that country "Athtar, the self-waterer, was a masculine deity. . . . In Egypt the Nile-God, Hapi, was a male and a father god."[52]

Also according to rabbinic sources, something of the terrible union between the male and the female waters which took place at the time of the great flood occurs every year in the rainy season on a scale reduced to harmlessness and with salutary instead of destructive effects. Rabbi Levi said:

The upper waters are male and the lower waters are female. And these say to those : Receive us, you are the creation of the Holy One blessed be He and we are his envoys. Immediately they receive them . . . like unto this female that opens before the male.[53]

Rabbi Abahu called the upper waters "bridegroom" and the lower waters "bride." He said:

When do we begin to recite the benediction over rain ?[54] When the bridegroom goes forth to meet the bride,[55]

I.e. when the waters accumulated on the ground rebound as rain-drops splash on them.

Other sages speak of the earth as the wife of the rain, which is the husband. Rabh Jehuda said:

Rain is the husband of the soil, as it is written, "For as the rain cometh down and the snow from heaven and returneth not thither except it water the earth and make it bring forth and bud."[56]

Rabbi Aha in the name of Rabban Shimeon ben Gamliel said :

Why is the early (autumnal) rain called *r'bhi'ah* (lit. : mating) ? Because it mates (*robhe'a*) with the earth.[57]

IV

We find in the Babylonian Talmud an interesting controversy between Rabbi Eliezer and Rabbi Joshua (end of the first century C.E.), who were fond of discussing cosmogonical and cosmological topics and who this time tackled the difficult question of the date of creation. The interesting point for us is that the statements of both sages are based on the assumption that the time of creation was a time of abounding fruitfulness, a sort of cosmic rutting season. Rabbi Eliezer said:

> In [the month of] Tishri the world was created . . . as it is written, " And God said, Let the earth bring forth grass, the herb yielding seed and the tree fruit. . . ." [58] Which is the month in which the earth brings forth grass and the trees are full of fruit ? You will have to say that this is Tishri, and that season was the time of the *r'bhi'ah* (the first rain, or, literally, " mating "), and the rains fell and [the plants] grew, as it is written, " And there went up a mist from the earth." [59] Rabbi Joshua said : Whence do we know that the world was created in [the month of] Nisan (*i.e.* March–April) ? Because it is written, " And the earth brought forth grass, and herb yielding seed after his kind, and the tree yielding fruit." [60] Which is the month in which the earth is full of grass and the trees yield fruit ? You will have to say, this is Nisan. That season was the period when cattle, beasts and fowls copulate with one another, as it is written, " The rams have mounted the sheep." [61]

Thus according to Rabbi Eliezer the creation of the world occurred at the time of the year when the autumnal mating of the rain with the earth takes place, that is, when a new generation of the vegetable world is conceived. According to Rabbi Joshua, on the other hand, the creation of the world occurred at the time of the year when the spring-time mating of the animal world takes place. Jewish tradition decided in favour of autumn as the season of creation, and fixed the completion of creation on New Year's day. In accordance with this, already in talmudic times the following sentence was said in the New Year prayers: "This day is the beginning of Your works, a remembrance of the first day."[62]

We have thus become acquainted with several mythological conceptions, the most relevant of which can be summed up as follows:

1 The creation of the world was preceded by the forceful separation by God of the upper male waters from the lower female waters. The waters resisted but were overcome.
2 Creation was also conceived of as a kind of cosmic rutting season, when the rain came down, mated with the earth and fructified it.
3 At the time of the deluge the male and female waters again united to destroy the world. The waters of the deluge issued forth from the spot on which later the Temple was built.
4 Each year when rain falls, the upper male waters unite with the lower female waters, like a groom with his bride.
5 The creation of the world took place in Tishri. The beginning of the yearly rainfall, in which something of the creation is repeated, is expected in Tishri.

Viewed against this rich mythological background, that rather enigmatic "lightheadedness" alluded to in rabbinic sources seems to be more in keeping with all the other rites of the great Jerusalem festival, each of which had the intent of procuring the blessing of fertility and especially the blessing of rain. We now suspect that the " lightheadedness " had something to do with the mythological conception of the natural phenomenon to bring which about was the purpose of the whole ritual.

Thanks to Mannhardt, Frazer, and others, we know that a very common method of promoting the fertility of the earth is the real or symbolic intercourse between the human sexes, on the fields or in temples, in seclusion or in public. "For," to quote the words of Frazer, " in the minds of many peoples at an early stage of culture the fertility of women is closely bound up with the fertility of the earth, and the same causes which promote or hinder the one are thought to promote or hinder the other, a ritual connection being supposed to subsist between the union of the human sexes on the one hand and the fruitfulness of the ground on the other."[63] From this symbolism arises also the abundance of obscene language and behaviour in sympathetic ritual, of which striking ancient examples are to be found in a Sumerian liturgy,[64] and in Greek, Roman, and Nabbataean rain-making rituals.[65] As Barton puts it :

> In countries like Babylonia and Egypt, where fertility depended upon the rise of the rivers, or like Palestine, where it depended on the rainfall, the flow of fertilizing waters was . . . thought of as the result of a divine sexual act—the marital union of a god and a goddess. In that stage of thought it would be equally natural that they should think that their deities could be encouraged to such a union by human examples. It is probable that at the religious feasts it was the

custom to indulge freely in such acts of union in order to encourage the deities to do likewise, that the fertilizing waters might flow, the earth be fertilized and fruits produced for the sustenance of mankind.[66]

V

We have already referred to the parallels between the temple festivities of Hierapolis and the Jerusalem feast of Water-libation. Now, the Hierapolis festivities were accompanied by licentious proceedings and orgies.[67] The myth and rites of Atargatis at Hierapolis were closely parallelled by those of Atargatis of Ascalon who, according to Albright, still survives to-day, in all probability, as the "Green Lady," *es-sitt el-Khadrā* or *Sittna al-Khadrā*. "In the spring the vernal equinox is celebrated by a procession to the sea, after which the unmarried youths and maidens of the village (ej-Jōreh) are said to bathe unclad in the surf.[68] Doubtless the prototype of this feast was a procession to the sea in which the image of the goddess was carried and bathed in the sea as at so many other places (among them in Hierapolis). In connection with this rite men and women probably bathed together and the lascivious held high carnival, as usual in the spring festival of the *dea syria*."[69]

It has repeatedly been said in this book that early religions were in the first place concerned with the material welfare of the people, the rituals serving to obtain tangible blessings for the community. In the next chapter, when returning to this question, we shall try to show that the material welfare of the people was thought directly to depend on the proper performance of the ritual. As in the whole Near Eastern area the welfare of the people ultimately depended on an adequate natural water supply, the great temple rituals of these countries were obviously performed with the same purpose in view, namely, to secure the annual water supply by bringing about either the fall of rain, as in Jerusalem and Hierapolis, or the rise of the rivers, as in Egypt and Mesopotamia. Though sameness of purpose does not invariably lead to sameness of means, we shall not be surprised to find a certain similarity also between the water-rituals themselves which were performed in the great religious centres of the ancient Near East. Such similarities, especially as appearing between the Jerusalem and the Hierapolis rituals and myths, have already been pointed out. We can but surmise that the licentious proceedings that were customary both to the north and to the south of Jerusalem also left their traces in the late Jewish ritual, the " light-headedness " referred to in rabbinic sources being their last survival ; to prove or disprove this by scientific argument would be extremely difficult.

VI

The same caution should be observed when attempting to relate the ritual beatings to the myths telling of the creator's struggle with the waters and his victory over them. Neither the myth nor the ritual contains any allusion to the other. The question whether the ritual beatings and other tumultuous actions were originally intended to be commemorative of the primeval struggle that preceded creation has thus to remain open.

There are, however, a few more points to be considered when looking for traces of the ritual combat in Jerusalem. The ritual combat may take the form of a foot-race. In the temple of Jerusalem such a foot-race took place daily between the young priests who wished to perform the task of removing the ashes from the altar. We read in the Mishnah:

> Originally whosoever (of the priestly family the turn of which fell on that day[70]) desired to remove (the ashes from) the altar, did so. If they were many, they would run and mount the ramp (of the altar) and he that came first within four cubits (off the altar) obtained the privilege. . . .[71] . . . it once happened that two were even as they ran to mount the ramp. One of them pushed the other who fell (off the ramp) and broke his leg.[72]

In the Tosefta and later sources we have another version of the incident between the two priests, the event taking on a tragic colouring:

> Our rabbis taught: It once happened that two priests were equal as they ran to mount the ramp, and when one of them came first within four cubits of the altar, the other took a knife and thrust it into his heart. . . . The father of the young man came and found him still in convulsions. He said, May he be an atonement for you. . . .[73]

Here again, as in connection with the "lightheadedness,'' we hear of an enactment on the part of the Law Court:

" When the Court saw that they incurred danger, they ordained that the altar be cleared only by count . . .''[74] which was a method of casting lots. The officer[75] would say to them : Raise the finger for counting, and would place them in a circular queue, take the mitre off one of them and name an arbitrary number. He would then begin to count from the priest whose mitre he had taken off, and proceed to count round and round the circle by the raised fingers, until he reached the number he had named. The priest on whom the number fell received the task.[76] But even this counting of the priests was a rather stormy affair ; to discourage priests who tried to cheat by lifting up both their forefinger and thumb, the officer would strike them with an Arab whip.[77] The picture we get from all this is that of a ritual race between young priests who in their zeal to obtain the privilege of cleaning the altar even let themselves be carried away to the extent of committing acts of extreme violence.

Another account, of a purely legendary nature in Judaism but reflecting actual races that were run in Byzantium, tells of a magnificent foot-race that took place in the Hippodrome of Solomon once a year, on the last day of the month of Kislew and on the first two days of the following month of Tebheth. Ten thousand youths of the quickfooted tribe of Naphtali[78] took part in the races, each carrying a golden shield.[79] The Hippodrome occupied an area measuring three parasangs by one. In the middle there were two rows of a sort of thicket into which were placed all kinds of beasts and birds, and around which the races were run eight times a day. Besides, there were two huge columns, on the top of each of which stood golden lions and from their mouths flowed all kinds of perfumes on to the people. The people were divided into fourfold and sevenfold divisions. Music was played: harps and flutes. The four parties of the spectators were dressed as follows: the king and his servants and the sages and their pupils, the priests and the Levites, were dressed in light blue garments, blue being the colour of the sky in autumn ; all the rest of Israel wore white, white being the colour of the snow which falls in winter; the people who came from the towns and villages of Palestine were dressed in red, red being the colour of the good fruit which ripens in summer; finally, the nations of the world who came from faraway countries to bring their presents to the king were dressed in green, green being the colour of the sea in spring when its waters are favourable for seafaring. The four colours of the people thus represented the four seasons.[80]

Here we have at least a definite statement as to the connection of the races with the seasons. Moreover, the races were held on the last day of Kislew and the first and second days of Tebheth, these three consecutive days approximating to the winter solstice as far as this is possible in a solilunar calendar like the Jewish.[81] It seems a safe inference that the golden shields carried in the races symbolized the sun, which begins its victorious race through the sky on the day of the winter solstice. This inference is strengthened by the Byzantine descriptions of annual races and circus-games, which show surprising similarity to the Jewish legend.

In the letters of Cassiodorus, who lived (end of the fifth and beginning of the sixth centuries) at the courts of Odoacer and Theodorich, we find a much fuller symbolic explanation of the circus: In the circus there are represented the changes of seasons,[82] the circuits of the sun and the moon, and the divisions of time into months, weeks and days, which are based upon them. The four colours of the factions (there were four δῆμοι, or factions of the charioteers in the circus) represent the four seasons: the green the blooming spring, the blue the cloud-covered autumn, the red the fiery summer, and the white the frost-covered winter. The twelve signs and the seven winning-posts correspond to the twelve months and the seven days of the week. The twenty-four races of six chariots each correspond to the twenty-four hours of the day and the night. The two-horse chariots imitate the course of the moon and the quadrigas that of the sun. The wheels of the chariots designate the borders of Orient and Occident; the water-ditch of the circus (the so-called *euripus*) is a picture of the streaming sea; the lofty obelisks point towards heaven. Thus the mysteries of nature were represented in the colourful variety of the public games.[83] From another author we learn that the significance of the contests was a prognostic one:

> Oinomaos (the mythical king of Pisaea in Elis [84]) introduced first the colours of the circus by which he represented, as it were, the combat of the earth and the sea. Lots were drawn. He to whose lot it fell to play the role of the earth, dressed in a green dress ; the representative of the sea, on the other hand, was clad in blue. This contest was arranged by Oinomaos on the 24th of March (the time of the vernal equinox). If the green colour won, all hoped the earth would be fertile ; if the blue won, seafaring was expected to be lucky. This is the reason why the land-dwellers wished for the victory of the green colour, while the seamen for that of the blue. [85]

Still another source gives even more details:

> It was Romulus who introduced circus-games in honour of the sun and the four elements, Earth, Water (Sea), Fire and Air. In the contest arranged by Oinomaos the seafarers and the inhabitants of the isles wished for the victory of the blue colour : its defeat would have caused storms, shipwrecks and poor fishing. The inhabitants of the dry land, on the other hand, wished for the victory of the green colour in order to be safe from bad crops and famine. . . . The circus itself was built according to the form of the universe. It represented heaven, earth and sea. Twelve doors represented the twelve signs of the zodiac, which determine the fate of the earth, the sea and human life. The surface on which the races took place depicted the earth, the water-ditch—the sea, the turning posts at the two ends—orient and occident, the seven running fields—the course of the planets, the quadriga—the four elements. . . . [86]

In the twelfth century C.E. these Byzantine games took place no longer on the day of the vernal equinox but on Christmas, that is, at the winter solstice, like the (legendary) races in the Hippodrome of Solomon in Jerusalem. It is the Jewish traveller Benjamin of Tudela to whom we owe this information. He writes :

> Close to the walls of the palace (in Constantinople) is also a place of amusement belonging to the king, which is called the Hippodrome, and every year on the anniversary of the birth of Jesus the king gives a great entertainment there. And in that place men from all the races of the world come before the king and queen with jugglery and without jugglery, and they introduce lions, leopards, bears, and wild asses, and they engage them in combat with one another ; and the same thing is done with birds. No entertainment like this is to be found in any other land.[87]

Even after this description of the cosmological significance of the Byzantine races, and the light it throws upon the Jewish legend of Solomon's Hippodrome, we can still say very little concerning the ritual significance of races in the Temple. The Jewish legend and the race of the priests to the altar, mentioned before, can serve to establish only the meagre fact that also outside the Sukkoth cycle races and competitions were known both in the Temple ritual and in legend.

It should not be left unmentioned that athletic games of a mythical-ritual significance were held in the ancient Near East at a much earlier period than the one to which the aforementioned rabbinic legends and Byzantine descriptions belong. In ancient Egypt one of the oldest and most important festivals was the king's jubilee. In the course of this festival, which was at one and the same time also the enthronement and New Year festival, ritual athletic games were held, " enacting the defeat of the enemies, a condition for the resurrection-enthronement."[88]

In the Babylonian *Akitu* festival a race took place through the streets as a symbol of the " glad tidings " of the resuscitation of the god.[89] Also in the Hittite Antakhshum feast there figured a race as well as a sham-fight. A class of court-officials ran a race with the king's chariot and the winner became " royal rein-keeper." This race has been interpreted by Ehelolf as a vegetation rite, and compared with the *lismu* of the *Akitu*, the Roman *robigalia*, and the Easter-race of the Teutons. The sham-fight was fought out between two parties, the Khatti and the Māsha people.[90]

In Northern Canaan, as far as the Ras Shamra texts allow of a reconstruction of the ritual:

> The fighting scene between Baal and Mot may have been performed in a rather realistic way, like the fights of the Osirian drama in Egypt. We may say, however, that the whole population of and around Ugarit lived through the drama in anxiety and with responsibility in bringing about first the victory of Mot and the death of Baal (the crops), and then of realizing the final triumph of Baal (the rain, the green, the cattle).[91]

Characteristically enough, the " immovable East " preserved down to at least the nineteenth century most, if not all, of the features comprised in the ancient Near Eastern and Byzantine New Year celebrations.

In Persia until recently the Nauruz, the New Year festival, was celebrated in a traditional manner that in its main features seems to go back to at least pre-

Islamic days. For the Nauruz is a solar festival retained within the lunar calendar introduced by Islam. It begins at the precise moment of the vernal equinox as calculated by the royal astronomers. There are many descriptions extant of this festival; we shall follow that of Jakob Eduard Polak who was the Shah's personal physician about the middle of the nineteenth century, and as such repeatedly witnessed the festivities from close quarters.

Some minutes before the Nauruz the Shah entered his great hall of audiences, his clothing studded from head to foot with glittering precious stones under the weight of which he could hardly move. He addressed a few words to the chief priests, who invariably answered him: "Beneath the shadow of your Majesty, who is the Asylum of the Faith, religion takes root ever more deeply, and the number of unbelievers diminishes day by day!" The Shah then would question the Great Vizier as to the state of the provinces, and receive the stereotyped answer that the rain and the mercy of Allah descended on to the fields, everything flourished under the Shah's blessed hand, and fullness and superabundance reigned everywhere—this notwithstanding the fact that in reality whole provinces might be suffering from dearth and famine. The Vizier's address would contain reports of the progress of the industries and arts, of victories of the glorious army, of the erection of bridges and caravanserais, of the construction of roads—even though there might be no war on, no building activities, and so on.

On the second day a great public audience was held in the great courtyard, attended not only by numerous officers and officials but also by colourfully decorated elephants, giraffes, and ostriches. When the Shah appeared between the " Carrier of the Shield " and the " Carrier of the Sceptre," an orchestra of some forty musicians burst into music and a volley of 121 guns was fired. When the Shah sat down on the " Throne of Suliman " all made obeisance to him, including the elephants. A formal dialogue would follow between the Shah and the Vizier, though in the terrible din they could not hear each other, since the Vizier stood at a distance of some sixty feet from the Shah. The Shah would inquire, for example, as to the state of security on the roads, and the Vizier would answer : " The weather is favourable and invites your Majesty to hunting expeditions." The Shah then would drink coffee and smoke a narghileh, his eldest uncle and the chief priest would say benedictions over him, and then the court poet would read out a lengthy poem extolling the Shah's physical beauty, strength, and valour, describing his victorious fights against lions and tigers, and his conquest of Rum (Constantinople), and exhorting him to subject also China. A courier would then be led in, clad in riding-habit and covered all over with dust, as if he had just arrived from a distant province, and would bring tidings of new victories over the Turcomans—even though there might be no war at all.

Half-an-hour later the public games would begin

in the great *maydan* (playground). The Shah would watch them from a window. On the playground athletes would fight and wrestle with one another, jugglers and buffoons would leap about on stilts, rope-dancers, harlequins, and clowns dressed up as lions or bears would bustle about. Real lions, tigers, and leopards would be led on leashes among the crowd ; monkeys would play their tricks, while the elephants and giraffes would just stand by. Rams would be incited to fight with each other. Afghan fighters would fight sham duels with shield and sword. And all the time an orchestra would be playing. In days past, obscene farces also used to be produced.

The feast of Nauruz lasts thirteen days, which are spent in reciprocal visits according to a strict etiquette. On the ninth or the tenth day, horse-races would take place. The Shah would send a few of his horses to participate in them, as would the princes, governors, and other high officials. The hippodrome had a circumference of half a *farsakh* (about two miles, or 3.36 km.), forming a circle divided by milestones into four stations. The horses would participate in three consecutive races : in the first race they would run six rounds, in the second four, and in the third two, *i.e.* altogether twelve rounds. Though the races would ruin many a good horse, care was taken that the horses of the Shah should invariably win the first prizes. During the pauses music would play and dancers entertain the public with lascivious jumps and pantomimes.

One circuit of the hippodrome would then be run in a relay-race by royal runners. According to an old tradition, on the last (thirteenth) day of Nauruz the houses were threatened with collapse, and therefore everybody would leave the town and spend the day in the gardens outside the city walls.[92]

This Nauruz festival, the ancient features of which will be readily recognizable to the reader, is an excellent example of the survival of ancient forms even though emptied of their original contents. What was in the ancient Near East, and even in Byzantium, the *dromenon* of a meaningful ritual, became in the modern Nauruz a popular entertainment, while the spoken part of the ancient ritual now became a polite exchange of greetings and a mode of complimenting and extolling the reigning Shah.

VII

Let us turn now to a rabbinic legend in which is mentioned yet another struggle between the Creator and opposing forces. Before God could create the world, he had first to banish the Ruler of the Dark:

> . . . in the hour when the Holy One blessed be He created His world, He said to the Ruler of the Dark : Get thee hence, for I wish to create the world in light. And the Ruler of the Dark is similar to an ox. In that hour the Holy One blessed be He said : Ruler of the Dark ! Get thee hence, and if thou dost not get thee hence I shall rebuke

thee, for I wish to create my world in light. . . .[93] In that hour the Ruler of the Dark said to himself: If I light up my darkness and hearken to him, I shall be a slave forever. I had better make myself as though I had not heard, and I shall [transgress] inadvertently and not wilfully. Immediately the Holy One blessed be He rebuked him. . . . When the Ruler of the Dark saw that the Holy One blessed be He rebuked him, he began to say before him: Lord of the World! Why dost thou want to create light before me? Said the Holy One blessed be He: If thou dost not get thee hence I shall rebuke thee and cause thee to perish from the world. . . .[94]

As we see, the struggle of God with the dark has been reduced in rabbinic legend to a bare minimum along the same line as the legend of God's struggle with the waters.

According to the biblical account the first thing created by God was light.[95] It is possible that the lighting of the tall candelabra was at some time held to be commemorative of this creative act. Moreover, light in biblical as well as rabbinic conception is the symbol of life and health, of joy and success.[96] The light created on the first day of creation, which is not identical with the light of the sun, the moon and the stars, which were created only on the fourth day,[97] is in the legends closely connected with the Temple. It was from the spot on which later the Temple was erected that the first ray of light issued and illuminated the whole world.[98] This light continued to emanate from the spot also after the Temple was built on it. Its source was the Holy of Holies in which the Holy Ark stood, and it lit up the Temple itself and shone forth through the windows. These windows were built not to let the light in from the outside, as windows usually do, but to let out the light from within. In accordance with this reversed function the form of the windows was also reversed. They were narrow on their inner side and widened towards their outer side.[99] Thus it would appear that the lighting of the great candelabra at the annual "Joy of the House of Water-Drawing" may have been even more than the commemoration of the first creative act; it may have represented the kindling anew of the cosmic light at its proper place, the Temple, the centre and source of the light of the world.

Nor was the cosmic significance of the Temple exhausted with the light that emanated from it. In the middle of the Temple, and constituting the floor of the Holy of Holies, was a huge native rock which was adorned by Jewish legends with all the peculiar features of an *Omphalos*, a Navel of the Earth. This rock, called in Hebrew *Ebhen Shetiyyah*, the Stone of Foundation, was the first solid thing created, and was placed by God amidst the as yet boundless fluid of the primeval waters. Legend has it that just as the body of an embryo is built up in its mother's womb from its navel, so God built up the earth concentrically around this Stone, the Navel of the Earth.[100] And just as the body of the embryo receives its nourishment from the navel, so the whole earth too receives the waters that nourish it from this Navel. The waters of the Deep crouch underneath the *Shetiyyah* stone at a depth of a thousand cubits, and down to them reach the *shitin*, the shafts, also created according to a legend in the days of creation.[101] Thus when the libations flowed down from the bowls on the altar into the shafts, they finally reached the waters of the Deep and could so fulfil their mission. They raised the level of the Deep, a task in which, as we have seen, they were assisted by the singing of the fifteen Songs of Ascents. Now, as the subterranean waters that supply the whole earth all issue from this place, the raising of the waters of the Deep here set the whole invisible irrigation system of the earth functioning. Quite a number of legends tell in an interesting variety of versions about this subterranean network of irrigation canals that issue from underneath the Temple and bring to each country its proper power to grow its particular assortment of fruits. If a tree were planted in the Temple over the spot whence a water-vein issued forth to a certain country, it would grow fruit peculiar to that country; this was known to King Solomon, who accordingly planted in the Temple specimens of fruit-trees of the whole earth.[102]

The waters that issued forth from the Temple had the wonderful property of bestowing fertility and health. Legends have it that as in days of old so again in the days of the Messiah "all the waters of creation" will again spring up from under the threshold of the Temple, will increase and grow mighty as they pour forth all over the land.[103] Water issuing forth from the Temple is a mythical picture already known from the new Sumerian period: On the cylinder inscription B of Gudea, which describes the sacred marriage between Ningirsu and Bau, we read that after its consummation water streams forth from a basin that is placed next to the couch of the gods, and brings henceforth abundance like the Tigris and the Euphrates.[104] According to Jewish legend the waters issuing forth from the Temple will divide into twelve streams corresponding to the twelve tribes of Israel, and " every field and vineyard which grow no fruit will be irrigated by these waters and they will bear fruit . . . and there, on the banks of the river, all kinds of fruit-bearing trees will grow . . . and they will bring forth their fruit each month anew . . . while these will be eaten those will bud forth . . . and whoever suffers of an ailment will take from their leaves and will be cured."[105] The ailments that the leaves of these trees will cure are especially dumbness and the sterility of women.[106]

Thus we have become familiar with two important features of the mythical picture of the Temple of Jerusalem. It is from the Temple that the light, the symbol of life and success, of health and joy emanate; and it is from the Temple that the waters pour forth bringing fertility to the world, to the vegetable kingdom as well as to man. In the next chapter we shall see that the smoke that rose from the altar on the Day of Atonement and the last day of the Feast of Tabernacles was also believed to indicate the course that the blessing of fertility would take during the ensuing year.

VIII

If it is from the Temple that the blessings of fertility issued forth to the whole world, within the Temple such blessings would of course prevail in an even more intensive manner. In order to understand the rabbinic legends in which this idea is expressed, one has to bear in mind that the temples of many an ancient people were regarded as the Nuptial Chamber in which the divine powers of fertility, the Father God and the Mother Goddess, celebrated their great annual wedding feast for the purpose of ensuring the fruitfulness of the earth and the multiplication of man and beast. From the new Sumerian period we have a description of the sacred marriage of the god Ningirsu with the daughter of heaven Bau. The warrior Ningirsu enters his temple like a whirlwind, Bau approaches him on his couch like the rising sun, and the union of the two provides abundance to Lagash just as the River Tigris when its waters rise high. After the marriage has been consummated and victory won over the enemies, Bau rests at the side of Ningirsu in the nuptial chamber.[107]

Again, Herodotus (Book I, § 181) tells of a sacred room at the top of the ziqqurat or stage-tower of the god Marduk at Babylon, where there was a richly adorned couch occupied by a woman " chosen for himself by the deity out of all the women in the land " and by the god who comes down in person into this chamber and sleeps upon the couch.[108] Such annual sacred marriages were also celebrated in various places in Egypt and other countries of the ancient East.[109] In ancient Canaanite ritual and myth too we have indications pointing to the sacred marriage.[110] In the sacred marriage the king or the high priest usually had the role of the male fertilizing god, and the queen or priestess fulfilled the role of the goddess. Also beyond the borders of the ancient East, *e.g.* in Greece, the sacred marriage, the ἱερὸς γάμος, was a prevalent ritual,[111] as also in many other more remote places. In ancient Hebrew religion, as Professor Hooke pointed out, "the element of the sacred marriage had been spiritualized in the form of the conception of Jahweh as Israel's husband."[112] Professor Oesterley tried to find a remnant of the nuptial chamber in the "booths" that the Bible prescribed as a dwelling-place for the duration of the seven days of the Feast of Tabernacles.[113]

We cannot here probe into the tenability of this view, for to do this it would be necessary to investigate the rich legendary material connected with the booths. We should, however, like to show that traces of the idea of the Nuptial Chamber can be found in quite another direction in ancient Jewish legends. In these, to put it briefly, it is the Temple, more accurately the Holy of Holies, which is represented as a Nuptial Chamber, though not until a comparatively late period do we find the express statement that the couple whose Nuptial Chamber it was, were God and the Holy Matrona personifying the Community of Israel.

The sexual principle in the Temple, however, is

alluded to in earlier rabbinic similes and legends. Let us begin with a simile which compares the Temple to a couch. The passage in the Song of Songs, " Behold his couch which is Solomon's"[114] is explained as alluding to the Temple:

And why was the Sanctuary compared to a couch? Because just as this couch serves fruitfulness and multiplication (*i.e.* sexual intercourse), even so the Sanctuary everything that was in it was fruitful and multiplied.[115]

It should be remarked that the Hebrew expression translated here, " fruitfulness and multiplication " (*piryah w'ribhyah*), is one commonly used to designate procreation. Another simile has it that the Temple was like a forest,[116] because " just as the forest is fruitful and multiplies, even so the Sanctuary, everything that was in it was fruitful and multiplied."[117] A legend gives us a clue as to the source of this wondrous property of the Temple: During the three months in which the Ark of the Lord was kept in the house of Obed Edom, each one of the wives of his eight sons gave birth to a child every two weeks.[118] It was the Ark, then, in which lay the power of fertility.[119]

In the Temple itself lifeless objects grew and expanded and the wooden parts of the building burst into leaf and brought forth fruit under the influence of the Holy Ark's presence. Solomon " planted " trees of gold in the Temple and these brought forth fruit which served as nourishment for the priests.[120]

The cedar [beams] which Hiram king of Tyre sent to Solomon for the building of the Temple scented the Life of the World and became green.[121]

Or again:

> Dry wood scented the Life of the World, blossomed, bore fruit and came to life.[122]

This " Life of the World " is none other than the Holy Ark:

> Rabbi Levi said: When Solomon brought the Ark into the Sanctuary, all the trees and cedar [beams] which were there became green and brought forth fruit. . . .[123]

According to another version this life-giving " Life of the World " was nothing else but the *Shekhinah*, the personified Presence or Glory of God.[124]

Likewise, the staves that were used to carry the Ark during the wanderings grew longer in the Sanctuary, until they reached the Curtain that separated the Holy of Holies from the Holy Hall before it and caused the Veil to protrude as the two breasts of a woman.[125] This prolongation of the staves occurred when the Ark together with the two Cherubs was placed in the Holy of Holies. At the same time also the wings of the Cherubs spread out, covered the Ark and hovered over the Sanctuary.[126] As to the Cherubs themselves, they were regarded as the central part in the Sanctuary, exceeding in importance even the Holy Ark:

> It is owing to their (the Cherubs') merit and the merit of their makers that the [holy] House stands. And they (the Cherubs) were foremost among all the things which were in the Temple, because it is upon them and upon the Ark that the *Shekhinah* rests. . . .[127]

The Cherubs depicted in a most tangible form the union between God and Israel:

Rabbi Qattina said: Whenever Israel came up to the Festival, the curtain would be removed for them and the Cherubs were shown to them, whose bodies were intertwined with one another, and they would be addressed: Look! You are beloved before God as the love between man and woman.[128]

As long as the people of Israel fulfilled the will of God, the faces of the Cherubs were turned towards each other like those of a loving couple to indicate that God loves Israel. But when the people of Israel did not fulfil the will of God, the Cherubs turned their faces miraculously away from each other, towards the walls.[129] We cannot here go into the implications of the legends in which the Cherubs appear as a Jewish counterpart of the widespread motif of the living statues,[130] nor can we do more than mention in passing that the Cherubs also bore the character of fertilizing winds.[131]

The most outspoken description ot the Temple as the Nuptial Chamber of God and the Matrona, the symbol of Israel, is found in so late a work as the *Zohar Hadash*, the "New Light," one of the foremost works of Jewish mystical literature in the Middle Ages. There we read that since the destruction of the Temple the Matrona descends night after night to the place of the Temple, enters

the place of the Holy of Holies, sees that her dwelling-house and her couch are ruined and soiled, and she wails and laments, wanders up and down, she looks at the place of the Cherubs and weeps bitterly, and she lifts up her voice and says: My couch, my couch, my dwelling-place . . . place of precious stones . . . in thee came unto me the Lord of the World, my husband, and he would lie in my arms and all that I wished for he would give me. At this hour he used to come unto me, he left his dwelling-place and played betwixt my breasts. My couch, my couch, dost thou not remember how I came to thee rejoicing and happy, and those youths (the Cherubs) came forth to meet me, beating their wings in welcome . . . how came to be forgotten the Ark of the Covenant which stood here. From here went forth nourishment unto all the world and light and blessings to all! I seek for my husband but he is not here, I seek in every place. At this hour my husband used to come unto me and round about him many pious youths, and all the maidens were ready to welcome him. And I would hear from afar the sound of the twin-bells tinkling between his feet that I might hear him even before he came unto me. All my maidens would praise and laud the Holy One blessed be He, then retire each to her place, and we remained in solitude embracing in kisses and love. My husband, my husband, whereto hast thou turned? . . . Dost thou not remember how thou heldst thy left arm beneath my head and thy right arm about me . . . and thou didst swear that thou wouldst never cease to love me, saying, "If I forget thee, O Jerusalem, let my right hand forget. . . ."[132]

One cannot fail to perceive that all this is elevated to a lofty spiritual plane, similar to that on which move also those Christian mystics who tell of their religious experience in terms of love between man and woman. It has repeatedly been pointed out that there exists a "tendency of religious emotion to express itself in the language of human love." This is common among the mystics. Thus St. John of the Cross, in "The Dark Night of the Soul," describes the mystic union in the following stanzas:

> On my flowery bosom, kept whole for Him alone, there He reposed and slept; and I cherished Him, and the waving of the cedars fanned Him.

As his hair floated in the breeze, that from the turret blew, He struck me on the neck, with His gentle hand, and all sensation left me.

I continued in oblivion lost, my head was resting on my love ; lost to all things and myself, and amid the lilies forgotten, threw all my cares away.[133]

The pictorial language both in these stanzas and in the passage quoted from the *Zohar Hadash* is essentially the same. The ideas expressed are identical too, with the exception of the representation of the Temple as the Nuptial Chamber, which is absent in the words of St. John of the Cross, and which precisely is the oldest element in the passage of the book of " New Light."

1 Cf. above, p. 29.

2 With the exception of the second, Ps. 121, which has " *shir lama'aloth*."

3 The teacher of David, cf. M. Aboth 6, 3.

4 Midrash Sh'mu'el, chapter 26.

5 B. Suk. 53a–b ; cf. B. Mak. 11a ; Gaster, *Sepher hama'asiyyoth*, 113–14.

6 Lucian, *De Dea Syria*, 13, ed. Strong and Garstang, pp. 51 sq.

7 Ex. 20, 2.

8 Y. Sanh. 29a bot.

9 Sode Raza, Yalqut Reubeni ad Gen. 1, 1, ed. Warsaw, 1889, vol. i, p. 4 sq.; cf. Hakham Harazim, Yalqut Reubeni ad Num. 26, 56, ib. vol. ii, p. 109.

10 Pirqe R. Eliezer, 31 ; cf. 23 ; Targum Yer. (Yon.) ad Gen. 8, 20.

11 Pausanias, *Descr. Graec.*, I, 18, 7.

12 Plutarch, *Sulla* 14 ; Etymologicum Magnum, p. 774, s. v. *ὑδροφορία* ; Hesychius, s. v. *ὑδροφόρια*.

13 Frazer, *Folk-Lore in the Old Testament*, London, 1919, vol. i, pp. 152 sq.

14 Gen. Rab. 32, 7, p. 294.
15 Gen. Rab. 13, 13, p. 122. Cf. B. Ta'an. 25b.
16 B. Ta'an. 25b.
17 Translation of Engnell, *Studies in Divine Kingship*, p. 140.
18 S. H. Langdon, *The Mythology of All Races*, vol. v. *Semitic*, Boston, 1931, p. 271; cf. p. 273.
19 *Annals of Ashurbanipal*, ed. R. J. Lau—S. Langdon, *Semitic Study Series*, ii, Leiden, 1903, 1, 45 sq. as quoted by Engnell, *Studies*, p. 44.
20 Gen. 7, 11 ; cf. 8, 2.
21 B. Ta'an, 25b.
22 A. Wiedemann, *Religion of the Ancient Egyptians*, London, 1897, p. 64 ; Erman, *Die ägyptische Religion*, Berlin, 1909, pp. 7, 8, 15.
23 Wallis Budge, *The Gods of the Egyptians*, London, 1904, ii, 103. According to the evidence of the Vedas, the Brahmanas, etc., also the ancient Indians conceived of the heaven and the clouds as a huge cow which fertilizes with rain the earth and the fields, cf. Gubernatis, *Die Thiere in der indogermanischen Mythologie*, Leipzig, 1874, pp. 37 sq. Also in German folklore the spirits of water and rain appear in the form of bulls and heifers, cf. *Handwörterbuch des deutschen Aberglaubens*, vol. ix, p. 133.
24 Schaeffer, *The Cuneiform Texts of Ras Shamra Ugarit*, London, 1939, pp. 63 sqq., 69, 70 sq.
25 Gen. Rab. 13, 6, p. 117. A similar idea is expressed by *Virgil, Georg.* ii, 324 sqq.
26 Schaeffer, *op. cit.*, p. 70.
27 Y. Ta'an. 64b mid. ; Y. Ber. 14a mid. ; Gen. Rab. 13, 13, p. 122 ; cf. Patai, *Hamayim*, p. 139 sq. ; id., *HUCA*, xiv, 261 ; id., *Man and Earth*, i, 123.
28 Y. Hag. 77a top ; c bot. ; Gen. Rab. 5, 2, p. 33 ; Ex. Rab. 15, 22.
29 Gen. Rab. 4, 5, pp. 28–29.
30 Is. 43, 16.
31 Midrash Konen, Jellinek, *Beth Hamidrash* ii, 25.
32 Gen. Rab. 5, 2, p. 33.
33 Pirqe R. Eliezer ch. 5 ; cf. Midrash Shoher Tobh, Ps. 93.

34 Job 26, 12 ; B. Bab. Bath. 74b.

35 Ex. Rab. 15, 22 ; Tanhuma Num. ed. Buber, pp. 97–98 ; Num. Rab. 18, 22 ; Cant. Rab. 15, 22 ; Midrash Wayosha', Jellinek, *Beth Hamidrash*, i, 46 ; B. Bab. Bath. 74b ; Midrash Shoher Tobh, Ps. 93, 5 ; Tanhuma Hayye Sarah 3 ; ib. Ḥukkoth 1 ; cf. also B. Hag. 12a ; Lev. Rab. 10, 9.

36 Gen. Rab. 5, 4, pp. 34–35.

37 Baraita di Ma'ase Bereshith, ed. Eisenstein, *Otzar Midrashim*, p. 317 ; Ze Ma'ase Bereshith, ed. Eisenstein, *op. cit.*, p. 315 ; Midrash 'Asereth Haddibroth, Dibbur 1 ; Midrash Haggadol, p. 26.

38 Gen. Rab. 20, 7, p. 190 ; cf. Cant. Rab. 7, 11 ; Midrash Haggadol Gen. ed. Schechter, p. 98 ; Yalqut Shime'oni, Cant. 7, § 992.

39 Seder Rabbah di Bereshith di Merkabhah, ed. Eisenstein, *Otzar Midrashim*, p. 314 ; cf. Pirqe Rabbi Eliezer, ch. 4. The quotation is Ps. 104, 7.

40 Is. 27, 1. B. Bab. Bath. 74b ; cf. ib. the similar legend on the Behemoth. Cf. Midrash Konen, Jellinek, *Beth Hamidrash*, ii, 26 ; Pirqe R. Eliezer, ch. 11 ; also S. Daiches, *Zeitschrift für Assyrologie*, vol. xvii (1903), pp. 394–99.

41 EGYPTIAN : Erman, *Die ägyptische Religion*, Berlin, 1909, p. 7, 14, 35 sq.; Wiedemann, *Religion of the Ancient Egyptians*, pp. 32 sq., 230 sqq. ; Wallis Budge, *Gods of the Egyptians*, ii, 96, 97 sq., 99, 100, 104 sq. ; Breasted, *History of the Ancient Egyptians*, p. 57 ; Jeremias, *Handbuch der altorientalischen Geisteskultur*, p. 23 ; Frazer, *Worship of Nature*, i, 70 sq., 355 sq. ; id., *The Golden Bough*, v, 283 ; Brugsch, *Religion und Mythologie der alten Aegypter*, Leipzig, 1885–88, p. 581 ; Hastings' *Encyclopedia of Religion and Ethics*, s. v. Earth. GREEK : Hesiodos, *Theogonia*, 517–20 ; Herodotos iv, 184 ; Strabo 17, 3, 2, etc. ; VEDIC : Tylor, *Primitive Culture*, i, 327 sq. ; Hastings, *op. cit.* ; CHINESE : Tylor, *op. cit.* i, 326, 328, ii, 272. POLYNESIAN : Tylor, *op. cit.* i, 322 sq., 325 ; Wundt, *Völkerpsychologie*, vol. v (1914), p. 417 ; Frazer,

Worship of Nature, i, 26 ; id., *The Golden Bough*, v, 283 ; AMERICAN INDIAN : Hastings, *op. cit.* s. v. Earth ; AFRICAN : Frazer, *Worship of Nature*, i, 96, 109, 627.

42 Cf. Albright, *Archaeology and the Religion of Israel*, Baltimore, 1942, p. 149.

43 Is. 27, 1 ; cf. Ps. 74, 14 ; Job 26, 13.

44 Is. 27, 1.

45 Is. 27, 1 ; Ps. 74, 13.

46 Syria, xvi, pp. 29–45 ; Schaeffer, *The Cuneiform Texts of Ras Shamra Ugarit*, pp. 65 sq. ; Millar Burrows, *What Mean These Stones*, New Haven, 1941, p. 268.

47 Book of Henoch 54, 7–10, ed. Charles, *Apocr. and Pseud.* vol. ii, p. 221.

48 Pirqe Rabbi Eliezer, ch. 23.

49 Leonard W. King, *Legends of Babylon and Egypt in Relation to Hebrew Tradition*, London, 1918, pp. 127, 128 ; cf. p. 53.

50 Morris Jastrow, Jr., *Sumerian Myths of Beginnings*, *American Journal of Sem. Lang. and Lit.*, vol. xxxiii, pp. 112, 113, 114. Cf. Barton, *Archaeology and the Bible*, 7th ed., Philadelphia, 1937, pp. 338 sq.

51 Cf. below, pp. 87, 88.

52 Wiedemann, *Religion of the Ancient Egyptians*, pp. 145–47 ; Barton, *Semitic and Hamitic Origins*, Philadelphia, 1934, pp. 139 sq.

53 Gen. Rab. 13, 13, p. 122 ; cf. Y. Ber. 14a mid. ; Y. Ta'an. 64b mid. Cf. also the saying of Rabbi Hama bar Hanina : " The day when rain falls is as great as the day on which the heaven and earth were created," B. Ta'an. 7b.

54 Cf. B. Ber. 54a.

55 B. Ta'an. 6b.

56 Is. 55, 10 ; B. Ta'an. 6b.

57 Y. Ber. 14a mid.; Y. Ta'an. 64b mid.; B. Ta'an. 6b. Cf. *Zeitschrift für alttestam. Wissenschaft*, vol. xxxiii (1911), pp. 81–83.

58 Gen. 1, 11.

59 Gen. 2, 6.

60 Gen. 1, 12.
61 Ps. 65, 14 ; B. Rosh Hash. 10b–11a ; cf. ib. 27a.
62 B. Rosh Hash. 27a. Cf. Pesiqta Rabbati, ed. Friedmann, p. 186b, where it is stated that the work of creation began on the 25th of the month of Elul, the month preceding Tishri, so that the seventh day of creation was the first of Tishri, that is New Year's day. Cf. also Seder 'Olam Rabba, ch. 4.
63 Frazer, *The Fasti of Ovid*, London, 1929, ii, 332. Of the vast literature on the subject let us quote here only a few instances : Frazer, *The Golden Bough*, i, 140 sqq., ii, 97 sqq., v, 39, 67, vii, 111 ; id. *The Devil's Advocate*, London, 1927, pp. 44 sqq. ; *The Worship of Nature*, i, 380 ; Dehon, *Memoirs of the Asiatic Society of Bengal*, Calcutta, 1, 9, 144 sqq. ; Hartland, *Primitive Paternity*, London, 1909, ii, 115 sq., 151 sq., 171, 210 sq., 236 sq. ; Crawley, *Savages and Sex*, London, 1929, pp. 41 sq. ; Briffault, *The Mothers*, London-New York, 1927, iii, 198 sqq. ; Dieterich, *Mutter Erde*, Leipzig-Berlin, 1925, pp. 97 sq., 146 ; Mannhardt, *Wald und Feldkulte* i, 480 sqq. ; Nyberg, *Kind und Erde*, Helsingfors, 1931, p. 240 ; Patai, *Man and Earth* (in Hebrew), ii, 124 sqq.
64 *Journal of the American Oriental Society*, vol. xli, pp. 143, 148. Cf. Cook, in Rob. Smith, *Religion of the Semites*, 3rd ed., p. 613 sq.
65 Hesiodos, *Opera et Die*, 391 sq. ; Virg. *Georgica*, i, 338 sqq. ; Maimuni, *Guide of the Perplexed*, part iii, ch. 37. Cf. Patai, *Man and Earth*, ii, 140 sqq.
66 Barton, *Semitic and Hamitic Origins*, pp. 160 sq., cf. also p. 112.
67 Lucian, *de Dea Syria*, 20, 50–53.
68 Cf. *Bulletin of the American School in Jerusalem*, no. 6, p. 16.
69 Albright, *American Journal of Semitic Lang. and Lit.* vol. xli (1925), p. 91.
70 Tos. Ta'an. 2.
71 M. Yoma 2, 1.
72 M. Yoma 2, 2.
73 B. Yoma 23a. Cf. Tos. Yoma 1, 12, p. 181 ; Y. Yoma

39d top. According to B. Yoma 23a the two incidents happened separately.

74 M. Yoma 2, 2.

75 Cf. M. Sheq. 5, 1.

76 M. Yoma 2, 2 and Rashi and Bertinoro *ad loc.*

77 B. Yoma 23a.

78 Thus according to Rabbi Yose ; Rabbi Johanan maintains that they were of the tribe of Gad.

79 Cf. i Kings 10, 17 ; 2 Chron. 9, 16, where it is told that Solomon " made three hundred shields of beaten gold." These shields must have had some ritual significance ; only so can we explain the promptness with which Rehoboam replaced them, and them alone, by brazen shields, when Shishak looted them together with all the treasures of the Temple and of the king's house, i Kings 14, 25–27 ; 2 Chron. 12, 9–10. Cf. i Kings 14, 28 ; 2 Chron. 12, 11 : " And it was so, when the king went into the house of the Lord that the runners bare them (the shields) and (later) brought them back into the chamber of the runners."

80 The Throne and Hippodrome of King Solomon, ed. Jellinek, *Beth Hamidrash*, v, 38 sq. Another symbolism of the four colours of the chariots, cf. Yalqut Shime'oni ad Zach. 6, 1.

81 These three days are the last three days of the Hanukkah festival, which in its origin seems to have had some connection with the Feast of Tabernacles, cf. Rankin, The Festival of Hanukkah, in Hooke, *The Labyrinth*, London, 1935, pp. 159 sqq. Also the Byzantine races, to be dealt with *infra*, took place according to a Jewish traveller of the twelfth century, at Christmas, cf. *The Itinerary of Benjamin of Tudela,* ed. Adler, London, 1907, pp. 12–13.

82 Cf. also Corippus 1, 17, as quoted by Ducagne, *Constantinopolis Christiana*, i, 102.

83 Cassiodorus, Variae Epistolae, III, 51. Quoted after Perles, *Monatschrift für die Gesch. und Wiss. des Judentums*, 1872, p. 125 ; cf. also A. Wünsche, *Salomos Thron u.*

Hippodrom, Ex. Oriente Lux, II, 3, Leipzig, 1906, p. 40.

84 Cf. Roscher, *Ausführliches Lexikon der griechischen und römischen Mythologie*, s. v. Oinomaos.

85 Excerpt from Greek manuscript historical collections, found in the notes of Nicolaus Alemannus to Procopius, *Historia Arcana*, c. vii, ed. Orelli, p. 333, as quoted by Perles, *op. cit.* p. 125.

86 Joannes Malalas, *Chronographia*, ed. Bonn, pp. 173–76, as quoted by Perles, ib. p. 126 sq. On the Hippodrome and circus in Byzantium see Charles Diehl, *Justinien et la Civilisation Byzantine au VIe siècle*, Paris, 1901, pp. 439–66.

87 *The Itinerary of Benjamin of Tudela,* ed. Adler, London, 1907, pp. 12–13.

88 Thausing, "Die Auferstehung im Sohne," *Wiener Zeitschrift für. die Kunde des Morganlandes*, xlvi (1939), p. 183, as quoted by Engnell, *Studies,* p. 11. As to the ritual combat in the annually performed religious drama at Edfu, cf. A. M. Blackman and H. W. Fairman, "The Myth of Horus at Edfu II," *Journal of Egyptian Archaeology*, vol. xxviii (1942), pp. 32 sq., 37.

89 Langdon, *The Babylonian Epic of Creation,* Oxford, 1923, pp. 52 sqq., Labat, *Le poème babylonian de la création*, Paris, 1935, pp. 42 sq., as quoted by Engnell, *Studies,* p. 65, n. 2. As for the foot-race in the Babylonian New Year festival between the demon Zu and the sun-god Ninurta in which Zu was defeated, cf. S. H. Hooke, *Myth and Ritual*, p. 9. Sham fights represented the fight of the king-god with the powers of chaos and his victory over them; cf. Engnell, *Studies*, p. 36, and Langdon, *The Mythology of all Races,* vol. v ; *Semitic*, Boston, 1931, p. 321.

90 Engnell, *Studies*, p. 65, quoting Eheloff, *Sitzungsberichte d. preuss. Akad. d. Wiss.*, 1925, pp. 267 sqq. and other authorities. Pedersen, *Israel*, vol. ii (1934), p. 550, refers to this sham fight as a parallel of the combat between Aaron and the Egyptian magicians as a part of the Easter-night ritual.

91 F. Hvidberg, *Graad og Latter i det Gamle Testamente,* Koben-

havn, 1938, p. 37, as translated from the Danish by Engnell, *Studies*, pp. 101 sq.

92 Jakob Eduard Polak, *Persien, das Land und seine Bewohner*, Leipzig, 1865, vol. i., pp. 367–89.

93 Pesikta Rabbati, ed. Friedmann, p. 95a.

94 *Op. cit.* p. 203a.

95 Gen. 1, 3.

96 Ps. 97, 11 ; Esth. 8, 16 ; Job 22, 28 ; 33, 28 ; Gen. Rab. 6, 3, p. 42, etc.

97 Gen. 1, 14–19 ; Gen. Rab. 3, 6, p. 21 ; ib. 11, 2, p. 89 ; 12, 6, p. 103 ; 42, 3, p. 418 ; B. Hag. 12a, etc.

98 Gen. Rab. 3, 4, p. 20 ; Midrash Shoher Tobh, Ps. 104 ; Tanhuma Gen. ed. Buber, p. 112 ; Pesiqta di Rabh Kahana 21, ed. Buber, p. 145b.

99 Tanhuma T'tzaweh 6 ; cf. B. Menahoth 86b ; Lev. Rab. 31, 7 ; Cant. Rab. 4, 4 ; Gen. Rab. 55, 7, p. 591 ; Y. Yoma 42c mid. ; Pesiqta di Rabh Kahana 21, ed. Buber, p. 145b ; Patai, *Man and Earth*, ii, 218 sq.

100 Jellinek, *Beth Hamidrash* v, 63 ; Seder 'Arqim, ed. Eisenstein, *Otzar Midrashim*, p. 70 ; Pirqe Rabbi Eliezer ch. 35 ; Midrash Shoher Tobh, Ps. 91 ; Zohar Num. vol. iii, p. 322, ed. Wilna. Also the Holy of Holies of Egyptian Temples was regarded as the mound that first rose from the primeval waters. Harold H. Nelson, "The Egyptian Temple," *The Bibl. Arch.*, Sept. 1944, p. 78.

101 Tos. Suk. 3, 15, p. 197 ; Y. Suk. 54d top ; B. Suk. 49a.

102 Tanhuma Lev. ed. Buber, p. 78 ; Yalqut Shime'oni Eccl. § 967 ; Eccl. Rab. ad Eccl. 2, 5 and Rashi *ad loc.* ; Siphre Deut. 37. Solomon planted also golden trees in the Temple, B. Yoma 21b, 39b ; cf. also Y. Yoma 41d ; Num. Rab. 11, 3 ; Tanhuma Num. ed. Buber, p. 33 ; Cant. Rab. 3, 9 ; Josephus, *Ant.* viii, 5, 2 ; Tanhuma T'rumah 11 ; Ahare Moth 8. According to Arab legends the four rivers of Paradise issue forth from beneath the Holy Rock in the Dome of the Rock, identical with the Shetiyyah Stone, Mujir ed-din, 205/6 ; Al-Musharraf, fol. 38 ; cf. Hartman, *Der Felsendom in*

Jerusalem, 1909, p. 10; Canaan, *Journal of the Palestine Oriental Society*, ix, 64 sqq.

103 M. Middoth 2, 6; Tos. Suk. 3, 3 and 10, pp. 195, 196; B. Yoma 77b–78a.

104 Franz M. Th. Böhl, *Zeitschrift für Assyrologie*, xxxix (1930), p. 91.

105 Pirqe Rabbi Eliezer, ch. 51; cf. Y. Sheqalim 50a top.

106 Y. Sheqalim 50a mid.; B. Menahoth 98a; B. Sanh. 100a; Cant. Rab. ad 4, 13. Cf. Wiesner, *Jahrbuch für Jüdische Volkskunde*, ii (1924–25), p. 77. On popular Jewish medicines for barrenness taken from the vegetable kingdom, cf. Patai, *Jewish Folk-Cures for Barrenness*, "Folk-Lore," London, Sept. 1944, pp. 117–24.

107 Franz M. Th. Böhl, *Zeitschrift für Assyrologie*, xxxix (1930), p. 91.

108 Jastrow, *Rel. of Bab. and Ass.* pp. 678 sq.; id., *Sumerian Myths of Beginnings*, *Amer. Journ. of Sem. Lang. and Lit.*, vol. xxxiii, pp. 118 sq.; cf. Gadd, in Hooke, *Myth and Ritual*, pp. 56 sq. On the "bedroom" in the Mesopotamian Temple cf. also Leo Oppenheim, "The Mesopotamian Temple," *The Bibl. Arch.*, Sept. 1944, p. 55.

109 Hooke, *Myth and Ritual*, pp. 9, 19, 34 sq.

110 Hooke, *op. cit.*, pp. 83, 85; id., *Origins of Early Semitic Ritual*, London, 1938, pp. 31, 33, 35, 38, 41. Cf. Engnell, *Studies*, pp. 131 sqq. where Engnell has a remark that may bear upon the "levity" in the Jerusalem Temple: "The divine marital union is of a rather "democratized" character, in being consummated doubtless by a number of priests and priestesses, but perhaps even by others—as rightly seen by Gaster. For this is indicated . . . also by the distinct 'ecstasy signs' among the female participants. . . ."

111 Cf. Frazer, *The Golden Bough*, ii, 143 n. 1; Harrison, *Themis*, Cambridge, 1912, pp. 91, 368; Chantepie de la Saussaye, *Lehrbuch der Religionsgeschichte*, 4th ed., Tübingen, 1925, vol. ii, p. 321; Patai, *Man and Earth*, i, 117, ii, 133.

112 Hooke, *Myth and Ritual*, p. 85.

113 *Op. Cit.* p. 139 sq.; in this contention he was endorsed by Hooke who compared the booths to the *gigunu*, supposing the latter, with Sidney Smith, *Jour. Roy. As. Soc.* 1928, pp. 849–68, to have been a chamber used for the ritual of the sacred marriage, cf. Hooke, *The Origins of Early Semitic Ritual, p.* 54.

114 Cant 3, 7.

115 Tanhuma Num. ed. Buber. p. 33.

116 Alluding to i Kings 7, 2.

117 Tanhuma Num. ed. Buber, p. 33; Num. Rab. 11, 3; B. Yoma 39b.

118 Y. Yeb. 6b bot.; cf. Num. Rab. 4, 20; Cant. Rab. 2, 5.

119 As to the actual role of the ark at its very beginnings, see J. Morgenstern, *The Ark, the Ephod and the Tent*, *Hebrew Union College Annual*, xvii (1942–43), pp. 153–265, and xviii (1943–44), pp. 1–52.

120 B. Yoma 21b, 39b; Y. Yoma 41d; cf. Num. Rab. 11, 3; 12, 4; Tanhuma Num. ed. Buber, p. 33; Cant. Rab. 3, 9; Josephus, *Ant.* viii, 5, 2.

121 Tanhuma T'rumah 11.

122 Tanhuma Ahare Moth 8.

123 Tanhuma T'rumah 11.

124 Tanhuma Ahare Moth 8.

125 Tos. Yoma 3, 7, p. 186; Num. Rab. 11, 3; Tos. Sheq. 2, 18, p. 177; B. Yoma 54a; B. Men. 98a–b; Tanhuma Num. ed. Buber, p. 33; Tanhuma Naso 11.

126 Baraita di M'lekheth ha Mishkan, ed. Eisenstein, *Otzar Midrashim*, p. 301.

127 Midrash Tadshe, Jellinek, *Beth Hamidrash* iii, 167.

128 B. Yoma 54a. Cf. ib. a–b: "Rabba bar Rabh Shilah said: Even as a man embraces his mate. Resh Laqish said: When the heathens entered the Temple and saw the Cherubs whose bodies were intertwined with one another, they carried them out and said: These Israelites, whose blessing is a blessing and whose curse is a curse, occupy themselves with such things! And immediately they despised them. . . ."

129 B. Bab. Bath. 99a and the commentary of Rashbam

ad loc.; cf. Introduction to Lam. Rab. § 9; Pesiqta di Rabh Kahana, 19; Yalqut Shime'oni ad Is. § 474.

130 Cf. Patai, *Man and Earth*, ii, 14 sqq.

131 Cf. *op. cit.* ii, 208 sqq.

132 Ps. 137, 5; Zohar Hadash, Midrash Ekhah, ed. Warsaw, n. d., p. 183.

133 Robert H. Thouless, *An Introduction to the Psychology of Religion*, Cambridge, 1936, p. 132.

he stretched out upon it the line of *Tohu*.'[34] 'And under the brim of it were knops '[35] corresponding to the three hundred and sixty-five windows which are in the east and in the west, out of one of which, in the east, the sun comes out, and sets in one in the west, '. . . the knops were cast in two rows ' these are the sun and the moon which compass the world round about and lead it. 'It stood upon twelve oxen ' these are the twelve constellations by which the world is governed. 'Three looking towards the north ' why is the north mentioned first ? Because it is open, because the north wind is open to the world, as it is written, 'He stretcheth out the north over the *Tohu* '[36] and, moreover, every evil wind comes from the north, as it is written, 'Out of the north the evil shall break forth.'[37] The Ram, Lion, Archer turn towards north, the Bull, Virgin, Goat turn towards west, the Twins, Balance, Water-Bearer turn towards south, and the Crab, Scorpion, Fishes turn towards east. 'And the sea is above upon them '[38] because the world is set upon the seas, 'and all their hinder parts were inward ' because they were created not for idleness but for the need of the world. 'And it was an handbreadth thick,' a handbreadth is five fingers, as the thickness of the firmament is a walking distance of five hundred years. 'And the brim thereof was wrought like the brim of a cup, with flowers of lilies,' as the heavens are wrapped round each other. . . ."[39]

We have quoted this lengthy passage in full in order to illustrate an exegetical method very common in rabbinic literature. Any idea could be given sanction by connecting it with a passage from the Bible. The connection could be quite arbitrary or superficial, such as a word, a number, or such like, shared in common by the biblical quotation and the idea propounded. Thanks to this method many an innovation made by individual sages and many an ancient popular tradition could be connected with the Bible and incorporated into rabbinic literature. In our case the ancient popular conception of the symbolic significance of the Temple was elaborated in every detail by giving each phrase in the biblical description of the Temple a cosmic interpretation.

A similar interpretation of the significance of the Temple is found in the writings of Josephus Flavius. In his *Antiquities of the Jews* we find the following equations:

1 The three parts of the Temple = the three parts of the world, namely: the court = the sea, the Holy House = the land, and the Holy of Holies = the heavens.[40]
2 The twelve loaves on the table = the twelve months of the year.[41]
3 The candlestick of seventy parts = the Decaniae, or divisions of the planets into tens.[42]
4 The seven lamps upon the candlestick = "the course of the planets of which that is the number."[43]
5 The veils composed of four things = the four elements, namely: the plain linen = the earth out of which flax grows, the purple = the sea, because purple is gained out of the blood of a shell-fish, the blue colour of the veils = the air, and the scarlet = the fire.[44]
6 The vestment of the high-priest was made of linen = the earth, blue cloth = the sky, pomegranate = lightning, and the noise of its bells = thunder.[45]

7 The ephaptis (*ephod*) = the universe made of four elements. The gold interwoven = the splendour of the sun.

8 The breastplate in the middle of the *ephod* = the earth in the middle of the world.[46]

9 The girdle of the high-priest = the ocean that surrounds the world.

10 The two sardonyxes on the shoulders of the high-priest = the sun and the moon.

11 The twelve stones of the breastplate = the twelve months, or the twelve signs of the zodiac.

12 The mitre, blue of colour = the heavens.[47]

To this in Josephus's *Wars of the Jews* is added :

13 " The altar of incense, by its thirteen kinds of sweet-smelling spices with which the sea replenished it, signified that God is the possessor of all things that are both in uninhabitable and habitable parts of the earth, and that they are all to be dedicated to his use."[48]

IV

Another interesting comparison, carried through in every detail, is that between the human body and the world. We cannot elaborate here this point, which we have had occasion to treat elsewhere[49] but another comparison based upon the two parallels man = world, and Temple = world, deserves to be mentioned here. The threefold comparison world = man = temple, is a favourite theme in ancient Indian speculation,[50] while in Pauline and medieval Christian thought we find only the comparison of man to the temple.[51] We have already seen that the two pillars

Jachin and Boaz were by Jewish legend regarded as symbolic of the sun and the moon. The same source makes these two columns correspond also to the eyes in the human body. " Just as the eyes are high and are placed in the head, even so were these two pillars high and thick."[52]

In another Jewish legend we read:

In the hour when the Holy One blessed be He said to Moses, Make me a temple, Moses said, How shall I know how to make it ? The Holy One blessed be He said, Do not get frightened ; just as I created the world and your body, even so will you make the Tabernacle. How [do we know] that this was so ? You find in the Tabernacle that the beams were fixed into the sockets, and in the body the ribs are fixed into the vertebra, and so in the world the mountains are fixed into the fundaments of the earth. In the Tabernacle the beams were covered with gold, and in the body the ribs are covered with flesh, and in the world the mountains are covered and coated with earth. In the Tabernacle there were bolts in the beams to keep them upright, and in the body limbs and sinews are drawn to keep man upright, and in the world trees and grasses are drawn in the earth. In the Tabernacle there were hangings to cover its top and both its sides, and in the body the skin of man covers his limbs, and his ribs on both his sides, and in the world the heavens cover the earth on both its sides. In the Tabernacle the veil divided between the Holy Place and the Holy of Holies, and in the body the diaphragm divides the heart from the stomach, and in the world it is the firmament which divides between the upper waters and the lower waters. . . .[53]

In another version of the same legend some additional equations are named:

In the Tabernacle there were fire and wind and water ; the offspring of the heavens is fire, the offspring of the air is the wind, the offspring of the earth is water. The fire is above and the water below, and the wind holds the balance between them. And in the body, the head is fire, the heart is wind (spirit) and the stomach water . . . "and thou shalt make a candlestick" [54] corresponding to the great light which was created on the first day in the world and was preserved in the body, as it is written, "The spirit of man is the candle of the Lord. . . ." [55] In the world there are seven stars which shed light and the world is in need of them ever since the seven days of creation, and in the body there are seven servants which are: the eyes, the ears, the nostrils and the mouth. And the following is to be stated concerning the three worlds. . . . The four-square of the altar corresponds to the foursquare of the world, east, west, north and south, "and the height thereof shall be three cubits" [56] corresponding to the three parts which are in man: the head and corresponding to it fire in the world, and the stomach and corresponding to it wind in the world, and the feet and corresponding to them water in the world . . . the altars were of gold and brass [57]. . . of gold corresponding to the soul, of brass corresponding to the body. Just as the gold is dearer than brass, even so the soul is dearer than the body; just as on the brazen altar offerings were made of the flesh of animals, even so day after day one offers to the body that which was allotted to it from heaven. . . . [58]

A more elaborate version of the last mentioned equations is found in the Midrash Tadshe:

The golden candlestick has seven lamps corresponding to the seven lights in the world which are the seven stars. In the year there are seven holy days, [59] in man there are seven gates, two eyes, two ears, two nostrils and one mouth. . . . The soul is within the body corresponding to the altar of incense which is within the Tabernacle. The Table is in the north corresponding to the Garden of Eden in which all sorts of pleasures are kept for the Righteous. The candlestick is in the south corresponding to the World to Come in which there is but the light of the Shekhinah (the Presence of God). There were there two altars, one of gold corresponding to the soul of man and one of brass corresponding to the body of man. . . . Just as the body eats, even so does the brazen altar whose offerings were food. And just as the souls do not enjoy anything but scent, even so nothing was offered on the golden altar but sweet incense, [a thing] which is done for scent. . . .[60]

In short, to use the succinct expression of Midrash Tanhuma:

The Temple corresponds to the whole world and to the creation of man who is a small world.[61]

One must on no account suppose that these symbolic interpretations are the result of idle speculation. Though we cannot in every detail demonstrate that all the parts of the Temple and its furnishings had a function corresponding to the symbolic significance attached to them, yet we are in a position to show this at least with regard to some of them. As to the altar, the foursquare of which corresponds according to one of the legends just quoted to the foursquare of the four cardinal points, we have already pointed out[62] that at least during the Feast of Tabernacles the altar covered with green branches represented the earth. This interpretation to which we arrived from the study of the role and function of the altar in connection with the Water-libation, is fully borne out by the earlier symbolism of the altar as the "*har'el*," the mountain of god. Albright has contended that this name is borrowed from the Sumero-Accadian

Arallu or *Arallû*, which has the dual sense of " underworld " and " mountain of the gods," the cosmic mountain. Cosmic mountain, *kursag* or *kur*, was the name also of the Sumerian temple-tower, just as *ziqquratu* means literally nothing else than mountain peak.[63]

The symbolic interpretation of the candlestick as the planets (Josephus and Midrash Tadshe) or the cosmic light which was created on the first day (Midrash Rabbi Shema'ya Hashoshani) is borne out by the ritual role of the great candelabra. The lighting of these, we have seen, was part of the ritual of the " Joy of the House of Water-Drawing," and, as we have found, represented the kindling anew of the cosmic light, the source of which was believed to be in the Temple. That the noise of the bells on the garments of the high-priest should represent thunder (Josephus) will not surprise us if we remember that we found sound-effects of a great variety as part of the rain-making ritual. These sound-effects are, in fact, often said to imitate thunder with the purpose of bringing it about.[64] The " pomegranates of blue and purple and scarlet " that hung with the bells round the hem of the priestly robe,[65] were said by Josephus to symbolize lightning. We do not exactly know what these pomegranates were made of, but we may be permitted to suppose that they were said to symbolize lightning because of the light flashing from them, just as Hiram, king of Tyre, was said by a Jewish legend to have imitated lightning by flashing precious stones one against the other.[66]

V

From the static aspect of the mythical significance of the Temple let us now turn to its dynamic aspect, and see in what manner was the Temple service interpreted as a means of securing blessings of welfare for the people.

The idea that the material welfare of the people depends on the proper performance of the ritual is a primitive one which survived also in higher forms of religion. The primitive tribe, to quote Wissler, "professes to believe that if the ritual is performed, something beneficial will follow. . . . Wherever we observe primitive rituals, this idea appears, not merely as our interpretation but in the expressed attitude of the participants. There seems, then, justification for the statement that one basic idea, but not the only such idea, in ceremonies, is the promotion of welfare, health, and long life by magic."[67]

Also in more evolved religions the same idea appears. In China the abandonment of the rigid and ceremonial cult of Shang-te, the heaven-god, was supposed to lead to "the ruin of states, the destruction of families, and the perishing of individuals."[68] In Indian Brahmanism "the rites of the religion are the real deities, or at any rate they constitute together a sort of independent and superior power, before which the divine personalities disappear, and which almost holds the place allotted to destiny in other systems. The ancient belief, which is already prominent in the Hymns, that sacrifice conditionates the regular course of things, is met with here in the rank of a commonplace, and is at times accompanied with incredible details."[69] The same holds good in the religion of Persia. Ahura Mazda said:

> If men sacrifice unto Verethraghna, made by Ahura, if the due sacrifice and prayer is offered unto him just as it ought to be performed in the perfection of holiness, never will a hostile horde enter the Aryan countries, nor any plague, nor leprosy, nor venomous plants, nor the chariot of a foe, nor the uplifted spear of a foe![70]

In the ancient Near East too it was the ritual that had to cope with the task of "securing the means of subsistence, to keep the sun and moon doing their duty, to ensure the regular flooding of the Nile, to maintain the bodily vigour of the king who was the embodiment of the prosperity of the community."[71] In the poems of Ras Shamra the ritual plays an important role. "Mourning for the death of the vegetation-god, rites to overcome his enemy, the god of death and the underworld, and to ensure the life-giving rains and the growth of the new year's crops, and rejoicing at the lamented god's restoration to life played a prominent part in these observances."[72] That the same attitude prevailed also in pre-Islamic Arabia can be gleaned from Himyaritic inscriptions. There we read of a people whose land was afflicted with hail and some other form of trouble, and who asked the god Almaqah, and were finally advised to perform certain ceremonies including the offering up of sacrifices. These proceedings were effective; the fields were saved from hail and the other plague.[73]

So too in the ancient western world. Among the early Greeks and Romans it was a principle that the religion of the State should be the religion of the people, as its welfare was supposed to depend upon a strict observance of the established cult.[74]

The common idea underlying all these beliefs is that the performance of the ritual assures the welfare of the people, mostly because the ritual was prescribed by a god, or gods, who rule supreme over the elements and forces of nature. If the ritual is performed according to the will of the god, he procures blessings for the people by means of these forces, while in the contrary case he contrives to use them to punish man. The single example of the ritual of Water-libation would suffice to show that this trend of thought is a secondary one, evolved, with the emergence of the gods, out of a more basic conception of the connection between ritual and welfare. When we see that the ritual acts, even in their late and evolved form, closely correspond to the phenomenon in nature to bring about which they are performed, we shall have to suppose that in their original significance such acts were aimed at the producing of the desired phenomena in a more direct way, by imitating or symbolizing the effect wished for, and thus appealing to sympathy in nature, or by forcing nature to yield with what Frazer termed "sympathetic" or "imitative magic." In rabbinic sources we cannot expect to find this idea clearly stated. We shall, in fact, find the idea of the omnipotence of God appearing everywhere between the ritual performances in the Temple and their effect in nature. Moreover, we shall not always be able to recognize the similarity between the ritual acts and the blessings brought about by them, at least not to an extent comparable to that of the Water-libation.

To begin with, the mere existence of the Temple had, according to legend, a beneficial effect on the functioning of the natural forces. Ever since the great flood, torrential rains fell forty days each year, and caused great damage to the earth. When Solomon built the Temple these torrents ceased.[75] Moreover, the structure of the whole world became firm only when the Temple was built:

> Rabbi Shemuel bar Nahman said: Before the Temple was built the world stood on a throne of two legs; but when the Temple was built, the world became [firmly] founded and stood solidly.[76]

Also the Jewish kingdom was firmly established by the act of the dedication of the Temple in the days of Solomon.[77] Again:

> In the days of Herod when the people were occupied with the rebuilding of the Temple, rain fell during the night but in the morning the wind blew and the clouds dispersed and the sun shone, so that the people were able to go out to their work, and then they knew that they were engaged in sacred work.[78]

As to the service performed in the Temple, most

of the rites were held to secure benefits that closely corresponded to the nature of the rites. Thus according to a saying of Rabbi Akiba:

The Torah said, Bring [an offering of] barley on [the feast of] Passover, because it is the season of the barley, in order that the crops should be blessed for you; bring [an offering of] wheat firstfruits on Pentecost which is the season of wheat, in order that the fruit of the trees should be blessed for you; pour water on [the feast of] Tabernacles, which is the season of rains, in order that the rains should become blessed for you. . . .[79]

As long as the sacrifices were offered in the Temple, the land of Israel had a wonderful fertility:

Rabbi Hiyya bar Abba (lived 3rd–4th centuries C.E.) said: When the sacrifices were brought, one measure[80] of Arbelian corn[81] when ground gave one measure of fine meal, one measure of flour, one measure of cibarium, one measure of bran-flour, one measure of bruised grain, and one measure of bran. But now, a man takes one measure of wheat to grind and does not bring back but the quantity he took along, and even a little less. Why? Because the presentation of the shewbread had ceased. See, how beneficial for them were the sacrifices which were brought upon the altar; for everything the kind of which was offered, brought blessing to its kind. . . . The bread of the commandments and the shewbread blessed the bread; the firstlings of the fruit blessed the fruit of the trees. It came to pass that Rabbi Jonathan ben Eleazar once sat under a fig-tree, and the fig-tree was full of beautiful figs. Dew fell and the figs exuded honey, and the wind kneaded them (the figs which dropped to the ground) in dust. There came a she-goat and from her dripped milk into the honey. And Rabbi Jonathan called his pupils and said to them: Come and see an example of the World to Come! And what was the reason for this [abundance]? That the sacrifices were being offered. It happened with a scribe who used to make the pilgrimage to Jerusalem every year, and the inhabitants of Jerusalem knew him to be great in [the study of] the Law. They said to him, Take [from us] fifty [pieces of] gold every year and stay with us. He said unto them, I have a vinestock which is more valuable to me than anything else. It gives me three vintages every year, making six hundred barrels every year. At the first vintage it makes three hundred barrels, at the second two hundred, and at the third one hundred, and I sell the barrels for much good money. And all this [abundance] is a praise of Jerusalem, because of the libations of wine which were offered [in the Temple] ; and when they ceased all these benefits were withheld. So you find that when Israel were in the exile in Babylonia, Ezra said unto them, Go up to the Land of Israel. And they did not want. So the Holy One blessed be He said, When you offered the shewbread you sowed little and gathered plenty, but now you will sow much and gather little. . . .[82]

Shimeon the Righteous, who was of the remnants of the Great Synod, used to say:

Upon three things the world rests : upon the Torah (the Law), upon the Service, and upon deeds of charity.[83]

To this utterance, contained in the Sayings of the Fathers, it is added in the complementary work of Aboth di Rabbi Nathan:

[The world rests] upon the service. This is the service in the Temple. And so you find that all the time that the service in the Temple was performed, there was blessing in the world, and the prices were low, and the crop was plentiful, and the wine was plentiful, and man ate and was satisfied, and the beast ate and was satisfied, as it is written, " And I will send grass in thy fields for thy cattle that thou mayest eat and be full."[84] When the Temple was ruined the blessing departed from the world, as it is written, " Take heed to yourselves that your heart be not deceived and ye turn aside. . . . And the Lord's wrath be kindled against you . . . and the land yield not her fruit."[85] And even so it is written, " And I called for a drought upon the land and upon the mountains,"[86] and so it is written, ". . . when one came to an heap of twenty [measures] there were but ten "[87] . . . and so it is written, " Ye have sown much and bring in little "[88] since the Omer (the offering of a sheaf of the firstfruit[89]) ceased. " Ye eat but ye have not enough "[90] since the shewbread ceased. " Ye drink but ye are not filled with drink " since the libations ceased. " Ye clothe you but there is none warm " since the garments of the priesthood ceased.[91] " And he that earneth wages earneth wages [to put them] into a bag with holes "[92] since the sheqalim (the yearly payment of one-third or one-half of a sheqel to the Temple[93]) ceased. And so it is written, " the fig-tree doeth not blossom "[94] since the firstfruit offerings ceased. " There is no fruit in the vines " since the libations of wine ceased. " The labour of the olive faileth " since the oil for the light and the anointing oil[95] ceased. " And the fields yield no meat "[96] since the wave offerings [of meat][97] ceased. " The flock is cut off from the fold "[98] since the continual burnt offerings[99] and additional offerings ceased. " And no herd is in the stall "[100] since the peace-offerings[101] ceased. . . .[102]

The sequel of the verses in Haggai upon which this passage is built, shows that the idea that it is the Temple upon which the fertility of the land depends was fully developed even before the Second Temple was built:

Thus saith the Lord of hosts, Consider your ways. Go up to the mountain, and bring wood and build the house . . . ye looked for much, and, lo, it came to little. . . . Why ? says the Lord of hosts. Because of mine house that is waste. . . .[103]

Rabbi Joshua made a statement to the same effect. His words are traditioned by Rabban Shimeon ben Gamliel:

Ever since the day that the Temple was destroyed there is no day without a curse, and no dew has fallen for blessing and the taste of the fruits has been taken away. Rabbi Yose said, Even the fatness of the fruits has been taken away.[104]

Rabbi Shimeon ben Eleazar said: The ritual purity which ceased caused the taste and smell of the fruit to cease. The tithe which ceased caused fat and corn to cease.[105]

So long as the service of the Temple exists, the world is full of blessing for its inhabitants, and the rains fall in their season, as it is written, ". . . to love the Lord your God and to serve him with all your heart and with all your soul. That I give you the rain of your land in his due season, the first rain and the latter rain. . . ."[106] And when the service of the Temple does not exist the world has no blessings for its inhabitants and the rains do not fall in their season, as it is written, "Take heed to yourselves that your heart be not deceived. . . . And then the Lord . . . shut up the heaven that there be no rain. . . ."[107]

"Raphram bar Papa in the name of Rabh Hisda: Since the day when the Temple was destroyed the south wind has never brought rain,"[108] though it is this south wind which should "bring up drops of rain and make the grass to grow."[109] And again: "Raphram bar Papa said in the name of Rabh Hisda: Since the day when the Temple was destroyed the rains no longer come down from the Good Storehouse"[110] in which God keeps the rains of blessing.[111]

VI

The service and the mere existence of the Temple assured, in addition to the proper functioning of the fertile powers of nature, a number of other benefits for the people. It warded off all kinds of catastrophes:

No conflagration ever broke out in Jerusalem, for the fire of the altar kept guard that no alien fire should break out. No collapse of houses ever occurred in Jerusalem, because the Shetiyyah Stone (the foundation stone of the world[112]) kept guard over all the building stones.[113]

The Tabernacle, the precursor of the Temple, assured not only material benefits but also spiritual blessings :

Rabbi Johanan said : Before the Tabernacle was built, evil spirits used to trouble the people in the world ; but when the Tabernacle was built and the Shekhinah (the Presence of God) sojourned below [in it], the evil spirits ceased from the world.[114]

As to the supposed function of the Temple furnishings, we have a detailed account:

" And he made ten lavers "[115] in order to increase the rains, as there was water in the lavers. Ten lavers correspond to the ten commandments. And why did Moses not make in the wilderness more than one laver ? Because Israel were in no need of rain in the wilderness, as the manna fell unto them and the well (of Miriam went everywhere) with them. Solomon made ten lavers in order to increase the rains, because (the Temple) was in an inhabited country and they were in need of much rain, as it is written, " a land of hills and valleys that drinketh water of the rain of heaven."[116] " And he made ten tables "[117] in order to increase the corn. And why did Moses only make one ? Because in the wilderness they needed no corn, and when Solomon came he made ten of them in order to increase the corn. " Five on the right side and five on the left,"[118] why so ? Because the south is called right and the left is called north . . . so he placed five on the right which is south, corresponding to the right side of the world whence the dews of blessing come to the world.[119] Solomon said: By the merit of these tables set on the right side there should come rains of blessing and dews of blessing unto the world from the right. And therefore he placed five tables on the left against north which is left, whence the evils come unto the world. Solomon said: Because of the merits of these tables set on the left, let the evils be withheld from Israel. In a similar manner he placed of the ten lavers five on the right and five on the left. "And he made ten candlesticks of gold"[120] corresponding to the ten commandments, and in each candlestick there were seven lamps, that makes seventy, corresponding to the seventy nations; for as long as the lamps burn the nations stay in submission, and since the day that the lamps became extinguished they rose and overpowered [Israel].[121]

In short the function of the Temple furnishings was believed to be as follows:

1 The ten lavers containing water ensured the fall of abundant rain.
2 The ten tables ensured the growth of abundant crops.
3 Five lavers and five tables on the right side attracted the rains of blessing and the dews of blessing from the south.
4 Five lavers and five tables on the left side withheld the evils which come from the north.
5 The seventy burning lamps kept in submission the seventy nations of the world, that is, ensured political security for Israel.

The nations of the world, on the other hand, enjoyed benefits unsuspected by them from the Temple service:

Rabbi Joshua ben Levi said: Had the nations of the world known how beneficial the Temple is to them, they would have surrounded it by camps in order to guard it. For the Temple was more beneficial to them than to Israel. For so Solomon fixed it in his prayer, "Moreover, concerning the stranger, which is not of thy people Israel, but is come from a far country for thy great name's sake, and thy mighty hand, and thy stretched-out arm ; if they come and pray in this house. Then hear thou from the heavens even from thy dwelling place, and *do according to all that the stranger calleth to thee for* ; that all people of the earth may know thy name, and fear thee, as doth thy people Israel, and may know that this house which I have built is called by thy name.''[122] But when he comes to speak of Israel, what is written? " . . . and render unto every man according unto all his ways, whose heart thou knowest.''[123] Solomon said, Lord of the world! If he be worthy, give it (his request) to him, and if he be not worthy, do not give it to him. . . .[124]

The parts of the priestly garments which, according to Josephus Flavius, were symbolic of parts of the universe, had according to talmudic sages an important ritual function :

Just as the sacrifices atone, even so the garments [of the priests] atone.

The coat atoned for bloodshed, the drawers[125] atoned for fornication, the mitre atoned for haughtiness, the girdle atoned for the sinful thoughts of the heart, the breastplate atoned for the transgressions of judgment, the *ephod* atoned for idolatry, the robe atoned for slander, the plate on the mitre atoned for insolence.[126]

In the previous chapter it was stated that the blessing was believed to emanate from the Temple in the forms of light and water. Another medium that was held to indicate the way of blessing from the Temple was the smoke of the pile of wood which rose from the altar both on the Day of Atonement (the tenth of Tishri) and twelve days later, on the

3 *Satapatha Brahmana* xiii, 8, 1, 17; 5, 2, 2; vii, 1, 1, 13. Cf. vii, 5, 1, 1 sqq. as quoted by Hocart, *Kings and Councillors*, p. 222.

4 Porphyry, *De Antro Nympharum*, 6, as quoted by Hocart, *op. cit.* p. 223.

5 Gray, *op. cit.* p. 152; Cook, *op. cit.* 54. On the *Ziqqurat* cf. below, p. 117.

6 G. Maspero, *L'Archéologie Egyptienne*, Paris, 1887, p. 88; Engl. Transl. 1895, p. 90, as quoted by Hocart, *op. cit.*, p. 224. Cf. J. Capart, *Egyptian Art*, London, 1923, p. 107.

7 Breasted, *Ancient Records*, iv, 219; cf. ii, 883; iii, 412, as quoted by Cook, *op. cit.* p. 54.

8 Plutarch, *Numa*, 11. Cf. Dionysius Halicarnassiensis, *Ant. Rom.* ii, 66, as quoted by Hocart, *op. cit.* p. 224.

9 Plutarch, *The Life of Romulus*, 11, as quoted by Hocart, *op. cit.* p. 224.

10 O. M. Dalton, *East Christian Art, A Survey of the Monuments*, Oxford, 1925, pp. 243 sq.

11 Cf. Jeremias, *Das Alte Testament im Lichte des Alten Orients*, p. 467.

12 Gray, *op. cit.* p. 152.

13 Num. Rab. 13, 19.

14 B. Suk. 51b.

15 Ex. 30, 18.

16 Ex. 25, 31.

17 Ex. 25, 20.

18 Gen. 1, 20.

19 Lev. 1, 2.

20 Yelamdenu fragment, ed. Jellinek, *Beth Hamidrash*, vi, 88; Yalqut Shime'oni, § 719; cf. Midrash Shoher Tobh, Ps. 26; Bacher, *Ag. Pal. Am.* iii, 3, ch. 17 at the end.

21 Cf. Jellinek, *Beth Hamidrash*, iii, p. xxxiv; Frenkel, Graetz' *Monatschrift*, xxv, 120, 330; Bacher, *Ag. Tan.* ii, ch. 18, on R. Pinhas ben Ya'ir.

22 Lev. 24, 6.

23 1 Kings 7, 21.

24 Ps. 89, 38.

25 Ps. 104, 19. In Hebrew seasons, *mo'adim*—feasts.

26 Ps. 19, 6.
27 Robertson Smith, *The Religion of the Semites*, 3rd ed. pp. 487 sq.
28 Albright, *Archaeology and the Religion of Israel*, Baltimore, 1942, p. 148, and also p. 139. Cf. R. B. Y. Scott, "The Pillars Jachin and Boaz," *Journal of Biblical Literature*, 1939, pp. 143 sqq.
29 Cf. above, p. 76.
30 1 Kings 7, 23.
31 Job 38, 38.
32 Job 37, 18.
33 1 Kings 7, 23.
34 Is. 34, 11.
35 1 Kings 7, 24 sq.
36 Job 26, 7.
37 Jer. 1, 14.
38 1 Kings 7, 25 sq.
39 Midrash Tadshe, ed. Jellinek, *Beth Hamidrash*, iii, 164 sq. Cf. Yalqut Shime'oni ad 1 Kings, § 185. In earlier times other interpretations were attached to the brazen sea and the twelve oxen, cf. Albright, *op. cit.* pp. 149–50 and notes.
40 Thus also in the Book of the Bee, cf. Grünbaum, *Neue Beiträge*, 39. The heaven was represented also by the throne of Solomon, cf. Wünsche, *Solomons Thron*, etc., pp. 2 sqq.
41 And the zodiac, Josephus, *Wars*, v, 5, 5.
42 According to Philo, *Life of Moses*, 3, 10, the candlestick is the symbol of heaven. Cf. Gray, *Sacrifice in the Old Testament*, p. 175.
43 Cf. Josephus, *Wars*, v, 5, 5. Cf. also ib. vii, 5, 5.
44 Cf. Josephus, *Wars*, v, 5, 4.
45 Cf. Josephus, *Wars*, v, 5, 7; Sap. Sol. 18, 24.
46 Cf. Josephus, *Ant.*, iii, 7, 5; Philo, *Life of Moses*, 2, 12.
47 Josephus, *Ant.* iii, 7, 7.
48 Josephus, *Wars*, v, 5, 5. According to Philo, *Life of Moses*, 3, 10, the altar of incense was the symbol of things on earth.

49 Cf. Patai, *Man and Earth*, i, 165 sqq.
50 Hocart, *Kings and Councillors*, pp. 64, 65, 228.
51 1 Cor. 3, 16; 6, 19; cf. Strack-Billerbeck, *Kommentar Zum Neuen Testament aus Talmud und Midrash*, München, 1922–1928, vol. iii, p. 335; Gulielmus Durandus, *Rat. Div. Off.*, Napoli, 1859, ii, 6, as quoted by Hocart, *op. cit.* 228.
52 Midrash Tadshe, ed. Jellinek, *Beth Hamidrash*, iii, 165; Yalqut Shime'oni ad 1 Kings, § 185.
53 Bereshith Rabbati, ed. Albeck, p. 32; cf. ib. additional sources.
54 Ex. 15, 31.
55 Prov. 20, 27.
56 Ex. 27, 1.
57 Ex. 27, 2; 30, 3.
58 Midrash Rabbi Shema'ya Hashoshani, ed. A. Berliner, *Monatschrift für die Geschichte und Wissenschaft des Judentums*, xiii (1864), pp. 227, 229, 230, 262.
59 New Year's Day, the Day of Atonement, the first and last day of the Feast of Tabernacles, the first and last day of Passover, and Pentecost.
60 Midrash Tadshe, ed. Epstein, *Miqqadmonioth Hayyehudim*, p. xxviii; cf. ed. Jellinek, *Beth Hamidrash*, iii, 175.
61 Midrash Tanhuma, Pequde, § 3.
62 Cf. above, p. 37.
63 Albright, *Archaeology and the Religion of Israel*, pp. 151–52; id., *Journal of Biblical Literature*, 1920, p. 137.
64 For instance, Kahle, *Palästina-Jahrbuch*, viii (1912), p. 162.
65 Ex. 28, 33–34.
66 'Inyan Hiram Melekh Tzor, Jellinek, *Beth Hamidrash*, v, 111; Yalqut Shime'oni, ii, § 367, ad Eze. 28. Cf. also Ginzberg, *Legends of the Jews*, vi, 424 sq., and above, p. 35.
67 C. Wissler, *An Introduction to Social Anthropology*, New York, 1929, p. 278.
68 Li Ki, vii, 4, 5 sq. as quoted by Westermarck, *The Origin and Development of the Moral Ideas*, London, 1926, vol. ii, p. 713.
69 Barth, *Religions of India*, pp. 47 sq., as quoted by Westermarck, *op. cit.*, p. 620.

70 Yasts, xiv, 48, as quoted by Westermarck, *op. cit.* p. 661.
71 Hooke, *Myth and Ritual*, Oxford, 1933, pp. 2 sq.
72 Millar Burrows, *What Mean These Stones?* New Haven, 1941, p. 236.
73 Corpus Inscriptionum Himyariticarum, 74, as interpreted by D. S. Margoliouth, *The Relations between Arabs and Israelites prior to the Rise of Islam*, London, 1924, p. 36.
74 Westermarck, *op. cit.* p. 648.
75 Tanhuma Gen. ed. Buber, p. 43.
76 Tanhuma Ex. ed. Buber, p. 94. Cf. Pesiqta di Rabh Kahana, ed. Buber, pp. 5b sq.
77 Aggadath Esther, ed. Buber, p. 29. Cf. Ginzberg, *Legends of the Jews*, iv, 40.
78 B. Ta'an. 23a, transl. Rabbinowitz, ed. Epstein, p. 115.
79 Tos. Suk. 3, 18, pp. 197 sq. Cf. Tos. Rosh Hash. 1, 12, p. 210; Y. Rosh Hash. 57b mid.; B. Rosh Hash. 16a.
80 In the original Hebrew *S'ah*, that is, appr. 12 litres.
81 Arbel was a village in Lower Galilee, to the north-west of Tiberias.
82 Tanhuma Ex. ed. Buber, p. 102–3; Tanhuma T'tzaweh § 13; Yalqut Shime'oni ad Hab. § 565; cf. B. Keth. 111b–112a; Y. Peah 20a bot.; Y. Sota 17b mid.; 24b bot.
83 M. Aboth 1, 2.
84 Deut. 11, 15.
85 Deut. 11, 16–17.
86 Haggai 1, 11.
87 Haggai 2, 16.
88 Haggai 1, 6.
89 Cf. Lev. 23, 10.
90 Haggai 1, 6, the continuation of the words quoted before. The passage is continued in the next two quotations.
91 Tanhuma Ex. ed. Buber, p. 103; Yalqut Shime'oni ad Proph. § 565.
92 Haggai 1, 6.
93 Neh. 10, 33. Cf. Ex. 30, 13.
94 Hab. 3, 17. The continuation of the verse is cited in the next two quotations.

95 Ex. 25, 6, etc.
96 Hab. 3, 17.
97 Ex. 29, 27.
98 Hab. 3, 17.
99 Ex. 29, 42.
100 Hab. 3, 17.
101 Ex. 24, 5 ; Lev. 3, 1, 6.
102 Aboth di Rabbi Nathan, version B, ed. Schechter, pp. 18 sq.
103 Haggai 1, 7–9.
104 M. Sotah 9, 12 ; cf. Tos. Sotah 15, 2, p. 321.
105 B. Sotah 49a ; Tos. Sot. 15, 2, p. 321.
106 Deut. 11, 13–14.
107 Deut. 11, 16–17 ; Aboth di Rabbi Nathan, version A, ed. Schechter, pp. 19–20, version B, ch. 5, pp. 18–19.
108 B. Bab. Bath. 25b.
109 B. Bab. Bath. 25a–b.
110 B. Bab. Bath. 25b.
111 Cf. Deut. 28, 12.
112 Cf. above, p. 85.
113 Aboth di Rabbi Nathan, 35, 1.
114 Num. Rab. 12, 3 ; cf. Midrash Shoher Tobh, Ps. 91 ; Pesiqta Rabbati 80, 5.
115 2 Chron. 4, 6.
116 Deut. 11, 11.
117 2 Chron. 4, 8.
118 2 Chron. 4, 8.
119 Cf. Pirqe Rabbi Eliezer, ch. 3.
120 2 Chron. 4, 7.
121 Midrash Tadshe, ed. Jellinek, *Beth Hamidrash*, iii, 164 sqq. ; cf. Yalqut Shime'oni ad 1 Kings, § 185.
122 2 Chron. 6, 32–33.
123 ib. verse 30.
124 Tanhuma Num. ed. Buber, p. 5 ; cf. ib. Ex. p. 93 sq. ; Num. Rab. 1, 3 ; in Lev. Rab. 1, 11 there is a similar legend concerning the Tabernacle.
125 A. V. : " breeches," Ex. 28, 42.
126 B. 'Arakhin 16a ; B. Zebahim 88b. A somewhat

different interpretation is found in Y. Yoma 44b bot. Cf. also Lev. Rab. 10, 6; Cant. Rab. ad 4, 1; Yalqut Shime'oni i, § 513.

127 Tanhuma Lev. ed. Buber, p. 60; Tanhuma 'Ahare Moth 3; Lev. Rab. 20, 4; Pesiqta Rabbati 190b.

128 B. Yoma 21b.

129 B. Bab. Bath. 147a; B. Yoma 21b. Weather auguries by means of smoke are practised to the present day by some peoples, f.i. the Swedes; cf. Mannhardt, *Wald und Feldkulte*, i, 509.

130 Jeremias, *Babylonisches im Neuen Testament*, pp. 62 sq.

131 Charles, *Secrets of Enoch*, xix, 6; xxi, 1; Test. Levi iii, 5; and his commentary on Rev. iv, 6; Cook, *The Rel. of Anc. Pal. in the Light of Arch.*, p. 54.

132 Ex. Rab. 35, 6; cf. ib. 33, 4.

133 Midrash Shoher Tobh, Ps. 30; cf. Gen. Rab. 55, 7, p. 591; Jellinek, *Beth Hamidrash*, v, 63; Eisenstein, *Otzar Midrashim*, 70, etc. A similar idea exists in Moslem tradition concerning the Ka'aba in Mecca, cf. Zamahshari ad Sura 52, 4; Ibn el Atir I. 28; Lane, s.v. *cataq* and s.v. *camarq*; Grünbaum, *Neue Beiträge*, 36.

134 Cant. Rab. 3, 10; 4, 4.

135 Mekhilta Beshallah, ed. Horowitz-Rabin, pp. 149–50.

136 On the significance of the blue colour cf. Patai, *T'kheleth, in Ludwig Blau Memorial Volume*, Budapest, 1938, pp. 174 sqq.

137 Num. Rab. 4, 13.

138 See above, p. 110. This is what is meant by the expression "the thickness of the firmament."

139 Gen. Rab. 69, 7, p. 797; cf. Midrash Sekhel Tobh, p. 142.

140 Seder 'Arqim, ed. Eisenstein, *Otzar Midrashim*, p. 70. Cf. Jellinek, *Beth Hamidrash*, v, 63. Allusions to this legend are found also in B. Hag. 12b; cf. Yalqut Shime'oni ad Wayishlah 33, § 132.

141 After a survey of the "cosmic significance of various parts of the construction and paraphernalia of the Temple

of Solomon " Albright remarks that this Temple " possessed a rich cosmic symbolism which was largely lost in later Israelite and Jewish tradition " (*Archaeology and the Religion of Israel*, Baltimore, 1942, p. 154). I think that in view of the material presented above, this sentence should now be modified.

Chapter Five

SINS AND CALAMITIES

I

We have seen in the previous chapters that in popular imagination the fall of rain was conceived of as a union between the male and the female elements in nature. We have also seen that the yearly fall of rain was assured by a great annual feast, the "Joy of the House of Water-Drawing." Among the ritual performances of this feast we believe that traces have been found of that ritual union between the human sexes which was supposed by a great number of peoples to be necessary for the inducement of a similar union between the elements. Many peoples who indulge in such a sexual liberty of ritual import, when celebrating the great marriage-festival of Heaven and Earth, obey during all the rest of the year the strictest rules in their sexual relationships. Just as on such ritual occasions it is prescribed to indulge in sexual liberty in order to promote the fertility of the fields, so on the remaining days any kind of illicit love is strictly forbidden, lest it damage the crops or cause other harmful reactions in nature. In many primitive cultures incest, adultery or fornication, which usually cover a much wider range of prohibitions than among civilized peoples, are regarded as the most serious crimes, and are believed to result in plagues, floods, droughts, famines or other calamities. Underlying this is the same belief in sympathy between man and nature on which rest also the Sacred Marriage and the ritual orgies. This belief in the reaction of nature has two complementary sides. On the positive side is the idea that the union of the human sexes is necessary in order to bring about the union of the male and female elements of nature. On the negative side we find the idea that man must refrain from illicit connections lest they cause illicit connections between the elements. Such illicit acts on the part of the forces of nature form the great natural calamities.

The analogy between the " illicit love " in society and that in nature is clearest in cases where human fornication is believed to cause storms, torrential rains and flood, which are regarded as illicit, unruly and unrestrained love between the male elements—such as the sky, the wind, the rain—and the female earth. Among the Sea-Dyaks of Borneo, for instance, " immorality among the unmarried is supposed to bring a plague of rain upon the earth as a punishment inflicted by *Petara*," the supreme being.[1] The Galelareese of Halmahera, a large East Indian island, believe that when it rains in torrents somebody is guilty of incest.[2] The people of Mindanao, in the Philippines, believe that incestuous unions cause floods.[3] The Old Catholics among the South Slavs believe that a village in which the seducer is not compelled to marry his victim will be punished with hail and excessive rain.[4] In India, torrential rains outside the rainy season are believed to indicate that too many marriages have taken place.[5] This last example, though it does not refer to fornication, yet expresses an idea belonging to the same trend of thought, namely, that excessive intercourse between the human sexes causes excessive intercourse between the elements.

These examples, drawn from all over the world, could be multiplied at will, but this would only be repetition. Let us instead turn to Jewish thought in which the analogy between fornication and the resulting calamity is expressed perhaps more clearly than anywhere else. We have heard already that in Apocryphal and rabbinic literature the great flood was regarded as the union between the upper male waters and the lower female waters.[6] This illicit and unnatural union between the two kinds of waters was brought about, according to the Midrash, by the illicit and unnatural sins such as paederasty and intercourse with animals, committed by the generation of the deluge :[7]

> The generation of the deluge was exterminated from the face of the earth through being immersed in fornication.[8]

Moreover, the sin and its consequent punishment had many sides in common: "Rabbi Yose ben Durmasqith said: They (the generation of the deluge) sinned with their eyes which are like unto water (by looking at strange women and inviting them to immorality), even so the Holy One blessed be He did not punish them but with water. Rabbi Levi said: They spoiled their seed (by having adulterous and unnatural connections), even so the Holy One blessed be He upset unto them the order of the world."[9] Rabh Hisda said: "They sinned with a hot thing (namely, the heat of fornication), and with a hot thing were they punished,"[10] namely, as Rabbi Johanan put it, "every drop of water that the Holy One blessed be He let fall on them, He boiled in hell, then brought it up and let it fall upon them."[11] So it happened that the hot waters of the Deep "scalded their flesh and flayed them. . . ."[12] Moreover "the waters of deluge were thick like the male *semen*."[13] The duration of the rain that accompanied the deluge had also its analogy in the sin that caused it. They spoiled by illicit intercourse the form of the embryo which develops into an animated being forty days after conception,[14] by causing women to conceive bastards, therefore the rains of the deluge fell forty days and nights.[15] On the other hand, during all the time that Noah and his wife, as well as his sons and their wives, spent in the ark, they had to abstain from sexual intercourse,[16] an interdiction which can be well understood if one keep in mind the Indian belief quoted above, concerning the influence of numerous weddings on rain.

The rabbinic material on this point could be amplified, and other points added, as for instance the very interesting idea found both in rabbinic sources and among other peoples, that also fornications committed by animals among themselves cause storms and floods. There is, however, no need to elaborate this point further.

II

The next point to consider is a seemingly contrary belief, that the sin of fornication causes drought. In this cycle of ideas the sympathetic connection between man's actions and the reaction of nature is less easy to discern. None the less, the principle is the same: a disturbance in society causes a disturbance in nature.

We may forego here to demonstrate by examples the working of this notion among various peoples; the notion that fornication causes drought and other disturbances in nature being by now a commonplace in anthropological literature. Let us only mention that were one to follow the method of the classical evolutionist school, the data concerning this notion would readily lend themselves to a developmental alignment. The primitive stage would be that in which the sin itself brings about the disturbance. At a later stage it would be the earth that punishes the offender and his community by withholding the crops. At a still later stage the earth would assume the character of an earth-goddess or an earth-god; and ultimately the god would emancipate himself from his earthly attributes and grant reward and punishment in accordance with his moral code.

In this book it has been my aim to collect from biblical and talmudic literature statements and passages in which one can still discern the belief in the direct influence of man's behaviour on the physical world. Such cases, however, of the working of sympathy between man and nature are relatively few, and to judge the character of biblical, midrashic and rabbinic literature according to them only, would be definitely erroneous. In order to avoid such a distorted impression, it is necessary to emphasize that the vast majority of the material preserved in biblical and rabbinic literature pertains to a stage in which man was believed to be able to influence nature only through the mediation of God to whom alone man is responsible and nature subject.

One of the few cases in the Bible in which direct influence over nature is attributed to man's doings is a passage in Job in which the suffering Job declares that he is innocent of adultery:

> If mine heart have been enticed by a woman, or if I have laid wait at my neighbour's door. Then let my wife grind unto another and let others bow down upon her. For this is an heineous crime . . . for it is a fire that consumeth to destruction and uproots all my crops.[17]

Here we have the familiar idea stated quite clearly: adultery uproots the crops, causes famine.

Less clear, but still worth mentioning in this connection, are the passages containing admonitions to the people of Israel not to commit incest, adultery, and other sexual transgressions, the consequence of which would be that "the land would vomit out her inhabitants."[18] The meaning of this phrase becomes clear when we compare it to other similar warnings, where the threatened punishment consists of the absence of rain and the famine following in its wake. It is in consequence of famine that the people are forced to leave the land, that the land vomits them out,[19] as it happened with Abraham, Isaac, the sons of Jacob, and Elimelech the father-in-law of Ruth.[20]

Also post-biblical Jewish literature yields ample evidence to the effect that fornication was regarded as the arch-sin, the greatest and gravest of all crimes, most hateful to God. In the Book of Jubilees we read, " and there is no greater sin than the fornication which they commit on earth. . . ."[21] The opinion that God shows patience and forgiveness to all crimes with the sole exception of fornication, or that God hates fornication, was expressed by a great number of talmudic sages.[22] Fornication was regarded as the cause of the destruction of Sodom and Gomorra,[23] and, according to Rabbi Simlai, it inevitably brings in its train great calamities in which the good and the wicked perish alike.[24]

It is interesting to note how the atonement for the arch-sin of fornication was alluded to in the ritual of Water-libation. In an earlier chapter it was pointed out that the wicks of the lamps lighted at the beginning of the festival were made of worn-out drawers and girdles of the priests. In the Jerusalem Talmud, which deals with this part of the ritual more closely, only the drawers of the priests are mentioned.[25] It is, moreover, stated there that from the worn-out drawers of the High Priest were made the wicks for the inner lamps, while those of the outer lamps were prepared from the drawers of ordinary priests. It would seem strange that such a minor detail as the stuff of which the wicks of the inner and outer lamps were made should receive so much attention. The answer is that these wicks too had their ritual significance. They were made of the drawers of the priest; and the drawers, we shall recall, were just that part of the priestly garments which was supposed to atone for fornication. Thus the use of the garments as wicks may have served to indicate that the arch-sin of fornication on account of which the rains might be withheld was duly atoned for, and its blighting power put to naught.

III

Although fornication was generally recognized as the arch-sin, disastrous effects on the order of nature were ascribed also to quite a number of other sins. The assumption that all kinds of grave sins lie at the root of any disturbance in the proper functioning of the natural forces, such as drought, famine, bad crops, pestilence, and so on is fundamental in the biblical doctrine of sin, though here too, as in the instance of fornication, cause and effect are mostly connected with each other only through the central link of the divine judgment. All the same it is still God who gives the rains and the crops, if the people deserve it. This is explicitly stated in a great many biblical passages,[26] and elsewhere the idea is implicit.[27] It is because drought and famine were regarded as the manifest proof of sins committed by the people that

Ezekiel speaks of the "disgrace of famine,"[28] and that the people, when perceiving that the cisterns were empty, were overpowered by a feeling not of despair, as we might expect, but of shame, so vividly pictured by Jeremiah.[29]

The same idea prevails in Apocryphal literature, from which let us quote only two passages, both from the Book of Enoch, to show the supposed disturbing effect of sins on nature:

> And in the days of the sinners the years shall be shortened,
> And their seed shall be tardy on their lands and fields,
> And all things on the earth shall alter,
> And shall not appear in their time :
> And the rain shall be kept back
> And the heaven shall withhold (it).
> And in those times the fruits of the earth shall be backward,
> And shall not grow in their time,
> And the fruits of the trees shall be withheld in their time.
> And the moon shall alter her order,
> And not appear at her time. . . .
> And many chiefs of the stars shall transgress the order (prescribed).
> And these shall alter their orbits and tasks,
> And not appear at the seasons prescribed for them. . . .
> And evil shall be multiplied upon them.
> And punishment shall come upon them,
> So as to destroy all.[30]

Now for the second passage: "Now, know ye that from the angels He will inquire as to your deeds in heaven, from the sun and the moon and from the stars in reference to your sins because upon the earth ye execute judgment on the righteous. And He will summon to testify against you every cloud and mist and dew and rain; for they shall all be withheld because of you from descending upon you, and they shall be mindful of your sins. And now give presents to the rain that it be not withheld from descending upon you, nor yet the dew, when it has received gold and silver from you that it may descend. When the hoar-frost and snow with their chilliness, and all the snowstorms with all their plagues fall upon you, in those days ye shall not be able to stand before them."[31]

Now as to rabbinic sources, here we find in addition to fornication quite a number of sins that are expressly stated by one or more of the sages to be the cause—or even the exclusive cause—of drought. Such sins are: idolatry, bloodshed, promises of charity which were not kept, the neglect of heave offerings and tithes, slander, insolence, the neglect of the Torah (the Law), and violent robbery.[32] We cannot here discuss each one of these sins and their harmful consequences in the working of nature. But there is a group of three sins, the harmful effects of which on the heavenly water-supply is emphasized in talmudic literature,[33] and which constitute the three cardinal sins. These deserve closer examination. The three cardinal sins are Idolatry, Fornication, and Bloodshed. These three cardinal sins constitute a special group within the religious precepts. "Rabbi Johanan said in the name of Rabbi Shimeon ben Jehozadaq: By a majority vote it was resolved in the upper chambers of the house of Nithza in Lydda that in every [other] law of the Torah if a man is commanded, 'Transgress and suffer not death!' he may transgress and not suffer death, excepting idolatry, fornication, and bloodshed.''[34] Idolatry, fornication and bloodshed defile the earth and cause the Shekhinah, the Presence of God, to withdraw.[35] These three sins caused the Temple to be destroyed.[36] They were conceived of as the three *tum'oth*, defilements, which had to be atoned for by the High Priest on the Day of Atonement.[37] The nature of the impurity attached to these sins and of their defiling effect was investigated by Buchler in his usual thorough and painstaking manner.[38] We need not therefore go into this matter all over again, but can instead directly tackle the question of how the ancient Jews conceived of the reaction of physical nature to these three cardinal sins.

IV

We have already spoken of the evil consequences of the second of these sins, fornication, and have adduced evidence to show that it was what could be termed the original sin. Idolatry, though it is persistently mentioned in the first place whenever the three cardinal sins are enumerated, is, when compared with fornication, secondary. The fact that in the Bible idolatry is constantly referred to, and pictured, as " whoredom,''[39] shows this clearly enough. As to the consequence of idolatry in the way of punishment effected through the forces of nature, it is expressly stated: " Take heed to yourselves that your heart be not deceived and ye turn aside, and serve other gods, and worship them; for then the Lord's wrath be kindled against you, and he shut up the heaven, that there be no rain and that the land yield not her fruit; and ye perish quickly from off the good land which the Lord giveth you."[40] It is more than probable that when talmudic sages, such as for instance Rabbi Yishmael, speak of idolatry as a sin that defiles the land,[41] they have this passage in mind, defiled land being a land that shows the signs of barrenness. In fact, when in the Jerusalem Talmud the sins that cause drought are enumerated, the sin of idolatry and its effect, drought, are included with reference to the above quoted passage. This conception of idolatry as a sin that causes drought found its ritual expression in the festivities of Water-libation, when the participants emphasized their innocence of precisely this sin, saying: "Our fathers who were on this place [stood with] their backs toward the Sanctuary and their faces toward the east, and they prostrated themselves eastward to the sun (that is, they practised idolatry); but as for us, our eyes are turned to the Lord (that is, we serve only God)."[42] When desiring to bring about a fall of rain, one would do well to declare one's innocence of one of the cardinal sins that cause drought.

The third cardinal sin, bloodshed, is well attested as a cause of other harmful reactions in the physical world besides the shutting up of the rains. The blighting effect of bloodshed on the fertility of the earth is reflected in the story of the first fratricide.

God said to Cain: "The voice of thy brother's blood crieth unto me from the ground. And now art thou cursed from the earth, which hath opened her mouth to receive thy brother's blood from thy hand. When thou tillest the ground, it shall not henceforth yield unto thee her strength. . . ."[43] Other biblical passages confirm that this is the result of polluting the earth by bloodshed.[44] This it is which has to be prevented by the performance of the rite of breaking a heifer's neck when the victim of an unknown murderer has been found.[45]

The belief in the blighting influence of bloodshed can easily be attested also from rabbinic literature. A legend has it that in the days of the creation all the trees had a wondrous fruit-bearing capacity. But when Cain murdered Abel, this fertility shrank and vanished.[46] According to another source, "When Cain killed his brother Abel all kinds of seeds and all kinds of trees which grew in the share of Abel the righteous, became blighted and sat in mourning and did not bring forth any fruit but fodder for the beasts . . . when Abel was killed the vine ceased to produce 926 kinds of fruit and nothing remained but one single kind. . . ."[47] Rabbi Jacob ben Nathanel tells in his *Book of Voyages* that in Caesarea there is the cave of the ten martyrs, the ten sages who were executed in connection with the revolt of Bar Kochba, and "no grass ever grows on the spot where these righteous men were killed."[48] The belief that grass will not grow on the spot where a man has been murdered is prevalent also among other peoples.[49]

V

Having now seen something of the sympathetic effect of the three cardinal sins, idolatry, fornication and bloodshed, on nature, let us go on to consider the expression of the supposed relationship between the sins of man and the reaction of nature. Of particular interest in this connection is the opinion of Rabbi Shimeon ben Yohai who supposed that there exists a definite correspondence between the behaviour of the people and the nature of the rain.

> Rabbi Shimeon ben Yohai said : If Israel were good on New Year, and plenty of rain was allotted to them, and finally they sinned, it is impossible to diminish the rains once the decision has been passed. So what does the Holy One blessed be He do ? He disperses the rains over seas and deserts and rivers, that the earth may not enjoy them. . . . If Israel were not good on New Year and little rain was allotted, and finally they repented, to add to the rains is impossible once the decision has been passed. So what does the Holy One blessed be He do to them ? He causes the rains to descend directly to the earth and causes dews to come and winds to blow with them, that the earth may enjoy them. . . .[50]

Elsewhere it is repeatedly stated that though sins are punished with drought, repentance can alleviate the situation. This was in accordance with the ancient ritual practice performed in the Temple and elaborated in later times. The first ten days of the year, from New Year to the Day of Atonement (1–10 of Tishri), are the " ten days of repentance." On the Day of Atonement the forgiveness of God is appealed to, and five days later the Feast of Tabernacles begins, which in its ancient ritual form was mainly devoted to the obtaining of the rains and the blessing of the fields.[51] What was thus performed in practice was succinctly expressed by the sages as a moral lesson in sayings such as, " The rains do not fall unless the sins of Israel have been forgiven,"[52] or, " When repentance ascends from the earth, immediately the rains fall,"[53] and the like.[54]

Just as fornication was not the only sin that affected nature, so drought was not the only ill consequence of man's wicked behaviour. In fact all the major misfortunes that befell Israel were attributed to their sins, to their transgression of God's commandments. In the following saying of Raphram bar Papa in the name of Rabh Hisda, the misfortune of insufficient rains appears as bound up with that greatest of all national catastrophes in the life of Israel, the loss of their native land: " While Israel fulfills the will of God, and Israel is on his own land, the rains come down from the good Storehouse (which is in heaven). But when Israel is not settled on his own land the rains do not come down from the good Storehouse."[55] Still other dread consequences are attributed to Israel's disobedience :

While Israel does the will of God and brings out his tithes as prescribed, " the eyes of the Lord thy God are always upon it (the land) from the beginning of the year even to the end of the year,"[56] and it (the land) does not suffer any harm. But when Israel does not do the will of God, and does not bring out his tithes as prescribed, " he looketh on the earth and it trembleth."[57]

But not only the blessings and punishment that come upon Israel are determined by the behaviour of the people; Israel is responsible for the very existence of the whole world. " Rabbi Hiyya bar Abba said in the name of Rabbi Johanan: . . . The earth said (in the hour when God gave the Torah to Israel), Say that Israel does not accept the Torah, and I shall return into my waters as I was. Thus also said Rabbi in the name of Rabbi Aha: . . . the world already was dissolving. Were it not that Israel stood before Mount Sinai (where the Torah was given) and said, 'All that the Lord hath said we will do and be obedient,'[58] the earth had returned to Tohu, to the void."[59] Of the numerous other sayings to the same effect let us mention the following:

" God said: Israel made peace between me and my world. Were it not for Israel, I would have destroyed my world." " When Israel accepted the commandment (which begins with the words) 'I am the Lord thy God'[60] the world became firmly founded." " All the benefits which come to the world come only for the merit of Israel. The rains do not fall but for his merit, the dews do not descend but for his merit."[61] " Were it not for Israel the rain would not fall unto the world, nor would the sun shine; only for the merit of Israel does the Holy One blessed be He give ease to the world."[62] ". . . even peace comes to the world only for your merit."[63] " The very families which live on the earth are blessed but for the sake of Israel . . . the very ships that sail from Gaul to Spain are blessed but for the sake of Israel."[64]

All the nations of the world are guarded by God for the sake of Israel.[65] The Sanhedrin, the Great Council, which holds its meetings in the very navel of the earth, protects the whole world.[66] And oppressed and persecuted Israel pleads before the nations of the world :

"Were it not for Israel, there would be no blessings in the world . . . were it not for Israel, the heavenly lights would not shine . . . and the rains would not fall. . . . And Israel said to the nations of the world : All these the Holy One blessed be He gives unto you for our sake and still you hate us. . . . I sacrifice seventy bullocks on the feast for the seventy nations and I pray for them that the rains may fall, but, alas, 'In return for my love they hate me!'"[67]

VI

Nothwithstanding the great variety of sins resulting in natural calamities, the fact remains that fornication was looked upon as the arch-sin, the sin most hateful to God, the one sin that He can never forgive.[68] If we bear this in mind we shall most readily understand the important role that children played, and still play, in the rain-making ceremonies of so many peoples.[69] The travellers and writers who tell of the participation of children in these ceremonies often fail to mention why precisely children take part in them. But when they do tell us of the reason for the children's participation, this reason is invariably stated to be the innocence of the children. In Arab and Oriental Jewish communities the children are taught to sing during the ceremony verses in which they stress their innocence. Among the fellahin of Palestine rain-processions take place in the streets of the villages. In Northern Palestine, in *Tibnin* for instance, boys and girls walk about in the streets, each carrying a stick to which is attached a rag which they dip into water. The adults sprinkle water on the children who sing:

Ya rabbina ya rabbina	O our Lord, O our Lord,
tib'a shite lizar'ina	give rain to our seed,
hinne kebār elaznabu	they are big who have sinned,
nehna zghār shū zambina	we are small, what are our sins ?

In *Kufr Abil* the children sing:

Ya rabběna ya rabběna	O our Lord, O our Lord,
ehna zghār esh zamběna	we are small, what are our sins ?
talabna khubz min umměna	we asked bread from our mother,
darbatna 'ala thummena	she hit us on our mouth.

The first two lines of this doggerel verse are sung also in many other places in Palestine.[70] In still other places the innocence of the children is taken for granted and only the sins of the village elders are stressed. In *Beit Jala*, in southern Palestine, when there is a drought, all the children assemble with much noise, and run from one street to another, beating empty tins and singing:

Ya rabbina ma tuakhidna	O our Lord, do not punish us,
kullu min mashāyihna	everything [bad comes] from our elders,
mashāyihna halikbār	our elders, the great ones,
ya rabbi tihriqhun finnār	O my Lord, burn them in fire !

Since the inhabitants of *Beit Jala* are Christians, the children also appeal to St. Nicholas:

Mār Inqula jīna lēk	St. Nicholas, we have come to you,
shukhb elmatar dākhil lēk	O stream of rain, I implore you,
w'ihna 'lyōm 'abīdak	we are to-day your servants,
muftāh assamā fīdak	the key of heaven is in your hand,
haiy imbū, haiy imbū	bring water, bring water !

Dr. Canaan who published these songs remarks that the word *imbū* is baby talk all over Palestine for "water." Let us also remark that some of the rain-processions are composed exclusively of children.[71]

Among the Arabs of Kerak in Transjordan almost exactly the same words are addressed to a saint of whom the Bible tells that he brought rain, namely Elijah.[72]

Among the semi-Bedouin of *Sawakhereh al-Wad* the oldest woman of the village is placed on the back of a donkey, in front of her a hand-mill which she keeps turning. She is led thus through the fields accompanied by a troop of village children carrying a cock which they torment in order to make it cry aloud. The old woman sings the rain-song, and the children shout the response which consists of almost the same words as those sung by the children of *Kufr Abil*, in which they stress their innocence.[73]

Such a procession with an old woman on donkey-back is arranged in many other places in Palestine as a rain-charm. The presence of the old woman in the rain-making ceremony gives a valuable clue to the nature of the sins the absence of which qualifies the children as rain-makers. The old woman, as Canaan observes, participates in the procession because she is *qat'a*, that is, free from menstruation, and therefore *tahrā*, pure.[74] A similar kind of purity, namely purity from sexual sins, is that which distinguishes here the children from the adults. To use Dalman's words, "the sinlessness of the old woman who can no longer sin and of the children who cannot yet sin " renders the request for rain more efficacious.[75] Thus we come once more to the same idea of fornication as the arch-sin that causes drought, and the absence of fornication as an absolute condition of the proper functioning of nature.

One might think that in respect of children it is their innocence in the broader sense of the word that is meant, and not necessarily innocence of sexual connections. But on examining the matter more closely, we soon realize that this impression is false. By " children " is generally understood boys and girls who have not yet reached puberty. Such children, and particularly the older among them, can and do commit all kinds of sins, such as lying, theft, robbery, and even bloodshed. The one sin that they are quite certainly incapable of committing is fornication. That this is the sin the absence of which makes children so efficacious in rain-processions, becomes even more clear when we find that old women whose sexual life is over are also held to have the same efficacy. For there is no doubt that as regards all other sins, such women are in no way different from other adults.

Let us now turn to the role of children in the rain-ceremonies of Oriental Jewish communities. In oriental countries in general the Jews have acquired, for one reason or another, a special reputation as rain-makers. Their rain-ceremonies are, in fact, often more elaborate than those of the surrounding Moslems. In Jewish rain-prayers the participation of children is a *conditio sine qua non*.

In Morocco the Jews send four children to the streets to march about holding the four edges of a white linen sheet. The children sing:

sabūla 'atshāna	the sheaf is thirsty
ghithha yā mulāna	water it, O our Lord!

and the people whom they pass pour water on the sheet.[76] In times of drought the children also sing:

O rain! fall! fall!
Richess is given by God.
His children are in the forest,
They call: "O father!
Buy me a shirt,
A shirt of carrots."
We have nothing to bite,
Nibble! nibble! Whatever can be nibbled.[77]

Among the Jews of Kurdistan, in Sineh, the skull of an ass is taken to the roof of a house and water is poured through it on to the ground. At the same time children collect pieces of wood, light them on the roof as a bonfire and throw the skull into it.[78] In Meshhed, in Persia, the prayers for rain are connected if possible with a circumcision ceremony. If in times of drought there chances to be a circumcision, the rain-prayers are said in the synagogue after the circumcision, while one of the supplicants holds the crying infant in his arms.[79] In the Caucasus, among the mountain-Jews, in times of drought, as Hahn reports, "children march round the churchyard several times and call upon Semirei, the god of rain."[80] Among the Yemenite Jews little school-children are called upon to pray to God for rain.

They are bid to sit on the floor in the middle of the synagogue, and the head of the synagogue addresses them as follows: "Holy seed (that is, children, the seed of Abraham), why are you silent, call strongly to our merciful Father, perchance He will listen to your voices and hearken to the breath of your mouths; the voice of the herd that has not sinned will reach the ears of our merciful Father." Yemenite Jewish children also used to have songs that contain requests for rain, and these were sung to their everyday games.[81]

A very similar role was already allotted to children in talmudic times in rain-requests. In the Babylonian Talmud it is related that "when the world was in need of rain the rabbis would send school-children to Hanan-who-hid-himself, and they would take hold of the hem of his garment and say to him, Father, father, give us rain! Thereupon he would plead with the Holy One blessed be He: Master of the universe, do it for the sake of these who cannot distinguish between the Father who gives rain and the father who does not give rain."[82]

VII

After this digression on folk-custom we can now view with more understanding the role that children played in the Feast of Tabernacles in Second Temple days. It was their purity that qualified them to perform the various functions, which negligible as they may seem at first glance had no doubt their ritual significance.

The first of these was the lighting of the candlesticks, which was performed by four "children of the flowers of priesthood," that is, priestly children. The meaning of the term "*pirhē k'hunah*," flowers of priesthood, is young priests,[83] but the Mishnah[84] in which the lighting of the candlesticks is described expressly states that it was done by "four *children* (*y'ladim*) of the flowers of priesthood." It is the children precisely, of whose ritual purity there can be no doubt, who have to perform the highly significant act of the lighting of the lamps, which was the beginning of all the festivities, just as the words "let there be light" were the beginning of the whole creation of the world.[85]

The second scene in which children are mentioned took place on the seventh day of the Feast of Tabernacles, after the altar had been beaten with the willow or palm-branches.[86] As soon as this was over, "the children quickly threw away their lulabs and ate their ethrogs."[87] Already the sages of the Talmud who lived but a few generations after the codification of the Mishnah,[88] no longer knew what exactly the children did on this occasion, as can be seen from the discussion on the subject. Later commentators, like Rashi and Obadia di Bertinoro, even held, in contradiction to the simple meaning of the text, that it was the adults who snatched away the lulabs of the children and ate the ethrogs of the children. What really happened becomes clear from a rabbinic legend telling of a pious man who gave his last pieces of money to charity and thus could not buy food for the last day of the feast :

> He was ashamed to go home, so he went to the synagogue and saw there (lying about) some of those ethrogs which the children threw on the day of Hoshana (that is the seventh day of the feast). . . . He took from them and filled his sack with them and went and sailed on the great sea (that is the Mediterranean) until he came to the city of the king. When he arrived there, it so happened that the king felt a pain in his intestines and they told him in a dream : Your remedy is to eat from those ethrogs which the Jews pray with on the day of Hoshana. At that hour they searched all the ships and all the towns and did not find. They went and found that man sitting on a sack. They said to him, Have you something (to sell) ? He said to them, I am a poor man, and I have nothing to sell. They searched his sack and found some of these ethrogs. They said to him : From where are these ? He said to them, From those with which the Jews pray on the day of Hoshana. They took the sack and brought it before the king. The king ate these ethrogs and recovered. They emptied the sack and filled it with golden denars.[89]

Let us combine the information contained in the Mishnah with that given by this story concerning the children and the ethrogs. The Mishnah reported that the children threw away their lulabs and ate their ethrogs. In this story we find that they threw at each other their ethrogs, which then remained scattered on the floors. The eating of the ethrogs thus seems to be reduced to a simple taking a bite into the fruit, which, as a matter of fact, is much too bitter in its unripe state in September-October to be really eatable. The picture that thus emerges from the only too meagre data is a joyful play of children throwing at each other their lulabs and ethrogs.[90] As to the ritual significance of this children's game we have to rely entirely upon analogous practices of other peoples, of which let us quote one prevalent in Morocco. At Aglu the food received by the participants in the rain-processions is finally handed over to a woman who has five or six children alive (that is, a woman who is particularly blessed), and she prepares it. The food is then eaten by the children of the village who have assembled in her house, nobody else partaking of the meal. It is believed that if the children play with the food, throwing it at one another, the year will be plentiful, whereas if they behave sedately at the meal the year will be bad.[91]

In talmudic times the children were regarded as one of the pillars upon which rest the existence and the welfare of Israel and the nations :

> Rabbi Abba bar Kahana said : There were in the world no philosophers (here meaning clever and cunning men) like unto Balaam the son of Beor and Oenomaus of Gadara.[92] All the nations of the world came unto Oenomaus of Gadara and said to him : Tell us, shall we be able to destroy this nation (Israel) ? He said : Go and make the rounds of their synagogues and schools, if you find there infants twittering with their voices you will not be able to harm them ; but if not, you will be able to harm them. For so has their Father promised them, " The voice is Jacob's voice but the hands are the hands of Esau "[93]—when Jacob is twittering in the synagogues, Esau (that is, the gentiles) has no hands (no power over them).[94]

What applies to the whole nation holds good also for each of its cities :

Resh Laqish said to Rabbi Jehuda the Prince : I have this tradition from my fathers . . . every town in which there are no school children shall be destroyed.

So, in fact, it happened with Jerusalem :

Rabh Hamnuna said : Jerusalem was destroyed only because school children ceased (from study).

According to another sage, Rabha, Jerusalem was destroyed only because " men of faith " ceased in it.[95] But as the children do not know sin, their merit is even greater than that of the " men of faith " or of sages who devoted their entire life to the study of the Torah :

Rabbi Shimeon ben Laqish said in the name of Rabbi Jehuda the Prince : The world exists only for the sake of the breath of school children. Rabh Papa said to Abbaye : And what of yours and mine ? He answered him : A breath in which there is sin is not like unto a breath in which there is no sin.[96]

There remains now for us to speak of the men of faith, the Pious and the Righteous, and of their place and role in connection with the order of the world. Of this we shall hear in the last chapter.

1 Westermarck, *The Origin and Development of the Moral Ideas*, ii, 675 ; Frazer, *The Golden Bough*, ii, 108 ; id., *The Devil's Advocate*, 47.

2 Frazer, *The Golden Bough*, ii, 111 ; id., *The Devil's Advocate*, 54.

3 Lord Raglan, *Jocasta's Crime* (Thinker's Library, No. 80), London, 1940, p. 10.

4 F. S. Krauss, *Sitte und Brauch der Südslaven*, Wien, 1885, p. 204, as quoted by Frazer, *The Devil's Advocate*, p. 98.

5 R. Briffault, *The Mothers*, London, 1927, iii, 199.

6 Pirqe Rabbi Eliezer, 23 ; Henoch 54, 7–10. Cf. above, chapter iii, p. 62. In biblical thought torrential rains and the flood itself are regarded as the expression of God's wrath, cf. Gen. 6, 6–7 ; Ez. 13, 11, 13 ; 38, 22.

7 Gen. Rab. 26, 5, p. 248 ; cf. Lev. Rab. 23, 9 ; Tanhuma Gen. ed. Buber, pp. 16, 24; Tanhuma Bereshith 12; also other sexual transgressions, cf. Gen. Rab. 31, 1–2, p. 270 sq.

8 Lev. Rab. 23, 9.

9 Gen. Rab. 32, 7, p. 294 ; cf. B. Sanh. 108a.

10 B. Sanh. 108b ; cf. B. Rosh Hash. 12a ; B. Zebahim 113b.

11 Gen. Rab. 28, 9, p. 267 ; cf. Y. Sanh. 29b bot. ; Lev. Rab. 7, 6; Eccl. Rab. ad 9, 4.

12 Pirqe Rabbi Eliezer, ch. 22 end ; cf. also Yalqut Shime'oni ad Is. 64, 1, § 508. Cf. also Ginzberg, *The Legends of the Jews*, v, 178, note 26 and the sources referred to there. As to the idea of " measure for measure " in connection with the sins of the generation of the deluge and their punishment, cf. ib. p. 183, note 42. The idea is expanded in the Zohar, Gen. 62a, 66a.

13 B. Sanh. 108b. Cf. B. Rosh Hash. 12a ; B. Zebahim 113b.

14 The belief that the embryo becomes a living being, " animatus," forty days after the conception, is an ancient Greek idea which penetrated into Christianity and Judaism. Cf. Aristotle, *De animalibus historiae*, vii, 3; Plinius, *Historia Naturalis*, vii, 6 ; Philo, *Questiones in Gen.* i, 25 ; ii, 14 ; St. Augustine, *Quest. in Exodum*, 80; *Quest. Veteris et Novi Test.* 23, Migne xxxiv–xxxv, 626, 2229 ; Gratian, *Decretum*, ii, 32, 2, 8 sq. ; Ephraim i, 149E, Ephr. Syri *Op. Omn.* ed. P. Benedictus and Assemanus, Roma, 1737–43 ; M. Niddah 3, 7 ; Tos. Niddah 4, 17, p. 645; B. Niddah 30b ; Tanhuma Num. ed. Buber, p. 29 ; B. Ber. 60a ; Num. Rab. 9, 1 ; Lev. Rab. 23, 12 ; cf. Ginzberg, *op. cit.* v, 106 sq.; Meir Aldabi (14th century), *Shebhile emunah*, iv; Preuss,

Bibl. Talm. Medizin, 451 sq.; Ploss-Bartels-Reitzenstein, *Das Weib*, i, 537 sqq.; Westermarck, *Moral Ideas*, i, 416.

15 Gen. Rab. 32, 5, p. 292.

16 B. Sanh. 108b; Gen. Rab. 31, 12, p. 286; ib. 34, 7, p. 316; 36, 7, p. 341; Y. Ta'an. 64d bot.; Pirqe Rabbi Eliezer, ch. 23; Tanhuma Gen. ed. Buber, pp. 42 sq.; Tanhuma Noah, 11–12.

17 Job 31, 9–12.

18 Lev. 18, 24–25, 27–28.

19 Deut. 11, 17; cf. Rashi ad loc., Targ. Onk. ad Lev. 18, 25; B. Sab. 33a.

20 Gen. 12, 10 sqq.; 26, 1 sqq.; 42, 1 sqq.; 43, 1 sq.; Ruth 1, 1.

21 Jub. 33, 20.

22 Gen. Rab. 26, 5, p. 249; Lev. Rab. 23, 9; B. Sanh. 93a, 106a; Lam. Rab. 5, 11. Cf. Ginzberg, *op. cit.* iv, 369 sq., vi, 404, n. 5. Cf. also Y. Ber. 13c mid., where an emphasis is laid upon the analogy between the sin of paederasty and its punishment.

23 Lev. Rab. 23, 9; Num. Rab. 9, 33; Y. Sota 17a.

24 Gen. Rab. 26, 5, p. 249.

25 Y. Suk. 55b mid.

26 Lev. 26, 3–5, 19–20, 34–36; Deut. 11, 13–17; 26, 15; 28, 4–5, 8, 11–12, 22–24, 38–40, 42; Is. 30, 23; Jer. 5, 23–25; 10, 13; 14, 22; 51, 16; Eze. 36, 29; Hos. 2, 23; Ps. 65, 10 sq.; 66, 9–10; 135, 6–7; 147, 8; Prov. 3, 20–21; Job 26, 8–9; 36, 27–28; 37, 6; 38, 25–28; 2 Chron. 7, 12–14; Sir. 43, 20 sq.; etc.

27 Jer. 3, 2–3; 12, 4; Is. 5, 10; 1 Kings 8, 35–36; 2 Chron. 6, 26–27.

28 Eze. 36, 30.

29 Jer. 14, 1–4.

30 Book of Enoch 80, 2–8, ed. Charles, *Apocr. and Pseud.* ii, 245.

31 Ib. 100, 10–13, ed. Charles, *op. cit.* ii, 272. Similar ideas are expressed also in 98, 6–8. Cf. also Hab. 2, 11.

32 Y. Ta'an. 66c mid.; B. Ta'an. 7b, 8b; B. Sabb. 32b;

Aboth di Rabbi Nathan. version B, ed. Schechter, p. 58a ; Mishle Rabtha 25. Such beliefs also exist among the fellahin of Palestine, cf. Kahle, *Palästina-Jahrbuch*, 1912, p. 163 ; Canaan, *Zeitschrift des deutschen Palästina-Vereins*, 1913, pp. 289 sqq. ; Dalman, *Arbeit und Sitte in Palästina*, Gütersloh, 1928–35, i, 133 sqq.

33 Cf. Y. Ta'an. 66c mid.

34 B. Sanh. 74a. Cf. Y. Sanh. 21b top.

35 Midrash Tannaim, Deut. 21, 23, p. 132.

36 B. Yoma 9b.

37 B. Shebu'oth 7b; Sifra ad Lev. 16, 16, p. 81c.

38 Cf. A. Büchler, *Studies in Sin and Atonement in the Rabbinic Literature of the First Century*, London, 1928.

39 For instance, Num. 15, 39; Hos. 1, 2, 7; Jer. 2, 20, 25; 3, 1 sqq.; Eze. 16, 15 sqq., etc.

40 Deut. 11, 16–17.

41 Y. Sanh. 26c mid.

42 Cf. p. 30.

43 Gen. 4, 10–12.

44 Cf. Num. 35, 33–34 ; Is. 26, 21 ; Eze. 24, 7 ; Job 16, 18.

45 Deut. 21, 1–9 ; cf. Patai, "The 'Egla 'Arufa or the Expiation of the Polluted Land," *Jewish Quarterly Review*, xxx (1939), pp. 59 sqq.

46 Tanhuma, ed. Buber, Introduction, p. 158.

47 Geniza-fragment in the Tylor-Schechter collection of the Cambridge University Library, published by L. Ginzberg in *Haggoren*, ix, Berlin, 1923, p. 66.

48 Cf. A. Ben-Yisrael, *Aggadoth Haaretz*, vol. ii, p. 193.

49 Cf. for instance, F. Legey, *The Folklore of Morocco*, London, 1935, p. 30 ; Patai, *Man and Earth*, i, 249.

50 Y. Rosh Hash. 57b ; cf. Siphre Deut. 40 ; B. Ta'an. 8b. Just the opposite concept is found in Matthew 5, 45.

51 Feasts of atonement before the beginning of the rains were celebrated also among other peoples, for instance the ancient Greeks, Gruppe, *Griech. Myth.* 162, and the Vedic Indians, Oldenberg, *Rel. d. Veda*, 319. Cf. also Volz, *Neujahrsfest*, 25.

52 B. Ta'an. 7b.
53 Y. Ta'an. 65b top.
54 Y. Ber. 9b top; Y. Ta'an. 63d top; B. Ta'an. 7b; Gen. Rab. 13, 14, p. 123.
55 B. Bab. Bath. 25b.
56 Deut. 11, 12.
57 Ps. 104, 32; Y. Ber. 13c mid.
58 Ex. 24, 7.
59 Pesiqta Rabbati 99b sq.
60 Ex. 20, 2.
61 Gen. Rab. 66, 2, p. 745.
62 Tanhuma Num. ed. Buber, p. 5; cf. ib. Ex. p. 93; Num. Rab. 1, 3; Deut. Rab. 7, 7.
63 Deut. Rab. 7, 7.
64 B. Yeb. 63a.
65 Siphre Deut. 40.
66 B. Sanh. 37a.
67 Ps. 109, 4; Midrash Shoher Tobh Ps. 109; cf. Pesiqta di Rabh Kahana ed. Buber, p. 193b sq.; Rab. 21 Num.; Tanhuma Pinhas; B. Suk. 55b; etc.
68 Cf. p. 146
69 Cf. Frazer, *The Golden Bough*, i, 250, 272 sq., 274 sq., 276, 278, 289; id., *The Worship of Nature*, i, 268, 274 sq.; I. Schapera, *Western Civilisation and the Natives of South Africa*, London, 1934, p. 28; Westermarck, *Ritual and Belief in Morocco*, London, 1926, ii, 256, 257, 259, 260, 264, 265, 267; Romanelli, *Massa' B 'arabh*, Warsaw, ed. Traklin, p. 68; Abela, *Zeitschr. d. deutsch. Pal.-Ver.* vii, 1884, p. 94. A. Musil, *The Manners and Customs of the Rwala Bedouins*, New York, 1928, p. 10: when no rain comes "the girls and wives of the Bedouins form a procession with the *umm al-ghejth*, mother of rain (Fig. 1, p. 13). A woman's gown is stretched over two sticks forming a cross and is carried by a girl (virgin) at the head of the procession which wanders from tent to tent, singing" (verses follow; no reference to children or to sins).
70 Kahle, *Palästina-Jahrbuch*, viii (1912), p. 163.

71 Canaan, *Zeitsch. d. d. Pal.-Ver.* xxxvi (1913), 290, 291; id. *Journal of Pal. Or. Soc.* xiv (1934), 67, 79.

72 Musil, *Arabia Petrea*, iii, 8. As to the rain-making of Elijah cf. above, chapter I, p. 43, and Patai, *Man and Earth*, ii, 145 sqq.

73 Hanauer, *Palestine Explor. Fund Quarterly Statement*, 1925, p. 35.

74 Canaan, *Zeitschr. d. d. Pal.-Ver.*, 1913, p. 292.

75 Dalman, *Arbeit und Sitte in Pal.*, i, 135; cf. ib. 136 sq. children's rain songs.

76 Oral communication of a Moroccan Jew in Jerusalem. Cf. similar cries among the Moroccan Moslems, Westermarck, *Ritual and Belief in Morocco*, ii, 265.

77 Brunot-Malka, *Textes Judéo-arabes*, Rabat (Maroc), 1939, pp. 98–99, 305, where there are given further children's songs sung at the times both of drought and of torrential rains.

78 Brauer, in *Magnes Anniversary Book* (in Hebrew), Jerusalem, 1938, p. 60.

79 Oral communication of a Meshhed Jew in Jerusalem.

80 C. Hahn, *Aus dem Kaukasus*, Leipzig, 1892, pp. 194 sq., as quoted by Frazer, *Aftermath*, London, 1936, pp. 91 sq. Dr. J. J. Rivlin suggested to me that Semirei may be a corrupt form of *Shabriri*, a demon connected with water, cf. B. 'Ab. Zar. 12b; B. Pes. 112a; Mekhilta Jithro 6.

81 Jacob Saphir Halevi, *Ebhen Saphir*, vol. i, Lyck, 1866, p. 107a; Brauer, *Ethnologie der jemenitischen Juden*, Heidelberg, 1934, p. 220; cf. Meyouhas, *Ma'asiyyoth 'am libhne qedem*, Jerusalem, 1938, p. 165.

82 B. Ta'an. 23b.

83 M. Middoth 1, 8; Y. Sota 17a top.

84 M. Suk. 5, 2.

85 The lighting of bonfires by children in the rain-charm of the Jews of Kurdistan is, by the way, not the only instance of the lighting of fire by children for ritual purposes. In a fertility rite in Lechrain, a high tree was set up which was lighted by children, cf. Mannhardt, *Wald- und Feldkulte*, i, 510. "Among the Ba-Ronga of

South Africa pottery is made by women only, and they prefer to employ a child under puberty to light the fire in which the pots are to be baked, because the child has pure hands and the pots are therefore less likely to crack in the furnace than if the woman lit the fire herself:" Frazer, *The Golden Bough*, ii, 204 sq., quoting H. A. Junod, "Les Conceptions physiologiques des Bantou Sud-Africains et leurs tabous," *Revue d'Ethnographie et de Sociologie,* i (1910), p. 147. Among various peoples of Negro Africa a sacred fire is tended mainly by small girls, less often by small boys. Cf. Tor Irstam, *The King of Ganda, Studies in the Institutions of Sacral Kingship in Africa,* Stockholm, 1944, pp. 33, 137, 139, 140.

86 M. Suk. 4, 6.

87 M. Suk. 4, 7.

88 The codification of the Mishnah took place about the end of the second century C.E. Cf. B. Suk. 46b.

89 Lev. Rab. 37, 2.

90 As to the duty of small children to use the lulab, it is expressly stated in Y. Suk. 54a mid., "as soon as a child is able to shake a lulab he is obliged (to perform the rite of the lulab)."

91 Westermarck, *Ritual and Belief in Morocco*, ii, 259.

92 Cf. Grätz, *Geschichte der Juden*, iv, 4th ed., p. 175, 434; Bacher, *Ag. Tan.* ii, 31 sq.; Blau, *Jewish Encyclopedia*, ix, 386, s.v. Oenomaus; Schürer, *Geschichte des jüd. Volkes*, 4th ed., vol. ii (1907), p. 55.

93 Gen. 27, 22.

94 Gen. Rab. 65, 20, p. 734 and parallel sources ib. Cf. the saying concerning the lamps of the Temple which while burning kept down the nations, p. 127.

95 B. Sab. 119b. About these "men of faith" we shall hear more in the next chapter.

96 B. Sab. 119b.

Chapter Six

FROM KING TO MESSIAH

I

In a previous chapter an account was given of the significance and function of the Jerusalem Temple according to popular imagination. When the Temple was destroyed, the natural order of things, which was in its entirety dependent on it, suffered a catastrophic disturbance. That this did not result in the extermination of Israel, nay, of all mankind, was due to the fact that besides the Temple Israel possessed another asset that made for the maintenance of the cosmic order, and this continued to function after the destruction of the Temple, perhaps even in an increased measure. This other beneficent influence emanated, according to popular belief, from the persons of the so-called "whisperers," "pious men," and " men of faith."

The belief that the welfare of the people depends on the behaviour and the qualities of a person who unites in himself both spiritual and political leadership is a very ancient one which is well attested among a great number of peoples. We now know for certain that in many instances the kingly office developed out of the profession of the tribal or village magician. The main original task of the priestly kings was the same as that which the magicians and medicine-men of primitive tribes are expected to perform to this very day, namely, to ensure the welfare of the people by making the rain fall, the sun shine, the fields yield their crops, man and beast be healthy and fruitful, and so on. If something went wrong, this was invariably ascribed to the misbehaviour or disability of the king. This is a great theme of which much has been written and of which still much could be said. Here can only be shown the working of this principle among relatively advanced communities, by means of three examples which, as far as I am aware, have not yet been utilized in this connection.

Philostratus tells in his *Life of Apollonius of Tyana* that in a conversation that took place between Apollonius and Domitianus, the sage offered to the emperor to enumerate the causes of pestilences. "But," continues Philostratus, "the emperor, fearful, I imagine, lest Apollonius should reckon among the causes of such epidemics his own wrongdoing, and his incestuous marriage, and his other misdemeanours, replied, 'Oh, I do not want any such answer as that.'"[1]

The second example is found in a sermon of Savonarola from the year 1491: "I must tell you, then," said this preacher of puritan piety, "that all the evil and all the good of the city depend from its head, and therefore great is his responsibility even for small sins, since if he followed the right path the whole city would be sanctified."[2]

The third example takes us to the Far East, to China. From the times of the third traditional dynasty there was preserved a collection called the *Great Law*, being a chapter of the famous Chinese Annals, and edited, according to Père Wieger, in the year 1050 B.C. This collection, which contains the traditional wisdom of many generations, is regarded as a sacred book. In this it is written:

> It is the duty of the government all the time to watch carefully the phenomena of nature, which are the echo in the world of nature of the order or disorder in the world of government. The government is bound to watch the phenomena of nature in order to be able immediately to amend what is in need of amendment. When the course of nature goes its proper way, it is a sign that the government is good, but when there is some disturbance in nature, it is a sign that there is some sin in the government. With the help of fixed tables it is possible to learn from the disturbance in nature what is the sin that caused it. Any disturbance in the sun accuses the emperor. A disturbance around the sun—the court, the ministers ; a disturbance in the moon—the queen, the harem. Good weather that lasts too long shows that the emperor is too inactive. Days which continue to be cloudy show that the emperor lacks understanding. Too much rainfall shows that he is unjust. Lack of rain shows that he is careless. Too great a cold shows that he is inconsiderate of others. Stormy wind—that he is lazy. Good harvest proves that everything is all right ; bad harvest—that the government is guilty. When the pear-tree blossomed in the autumn, the court had to be warned that there was some hidden disorder there. . . .[3]

Père Wieger, from whose book on Chinese religious beliefs and philosophical opinions we take this quotation, remarks in conclusion that the belief expressed in this passage left its traces in Chinese history from the third dynasty and down to the twentieth century.

Before turning to the ancient Hebrews, it should be observed that the notion of the kings as responsible for the material welfare of their peoples was prevalent in the ancient Near East in general. In an enthronement hymn from the time of Merneptah we read:

Rejoice, thou entire land : the goodly time has come. . . .
The water standeth and faileth not, the Nile is running high.
The days are long, the nights have hours, the months come aright.[4]

Pharaoh was hailed as " lord of flood, plentiful in grain, in whose footsteps is the harvest goddess," etc.[5]

It was a familiar feature of the Assyro-Babylonian religion that the king was held responsible, to the extent of being sometimes severely punished, for any calamity that descended upon his people.[6] The good king's rulership, on the other hand, means good crops.[7] In a blessing of Esarhaddon we find:

The kingship as the plant of life may be good for the welfare of the people.[8]

The gods granted to Esarhaddon

" abundant rains, copious inundations, acceptable prices ; old men dance, young men sing; matrons, maidens are gay with laughter; men take wives, they bring about the births; they bring sons and daughters to birth, reproduction is prosperous; . . . those who have been sick many days regain life; the hungry are satisfied, the lean grow fat, the destitute are supplied with clothing." [9]

In a hymn to Shulgi the king is addressed as " he that overfloweth the face of the country with the water flood."[10] Another king is allotted the task by Anu " to subjugate the enemy's country, make firm the fundament of the land; years of abundance, a reign of remote days [he has been granted]."[11] Nebuchadrezzar says of himself:

A reign of abundance, years of exuberance in my country I cause to be.[12]

With Assurbanipal's ascension to the throne

Adad let loose his showers, Ea opened his fountains, the corn grew five ells high in its ear (straw ?), the spike became five-sixths of an ell, the harvest was good, (there was) fulness of Nisaba, the giparu-tree was ever-bearing, the fruit-trees brought the fruit to luxuriant issue ; the cattle were prosperous in parturition ; in my reign exuberance superabounds, in my years superfluity is heaped up.[13]

As remarked already by Père Dhorme, this passage has a distinct messianic flavour[14]; and, as we shall see towards the end of this chapter, the same sort of messianism, projected, it is true, to the future, occurs also in rabbinic literature.

Other texts depict the social benefits enjoyed by the people under Assurbanipal: no force, no injury, security on the roads, no bloodshed, no outrage, general peace.[15]

In a Hittite text we read that Murshilish says about his father: " . . . under him the whole land of Khatti prospered, and in his time people, cattle, sheep multiplied."[16]

Also in the West-Semitic world the king is assigned a similar role. According to a Tell el-Amarna letter " the earth sprouts forth " at the king's word.[17] The king gives richess, sheep, flock, cattle, silver, gold and byssos to his subjects, and there is no maltreatment under his rule.[18] As to the Ras Shamra texts, Virolleaud had stated that Dan'el is a divine king, with power over the crops.[19]

II

To turn now to the Jews, the belief that the orderly functioning of nature and the welfare of the people depend on a central personality is discernible in biblical as well as in talmudic times. In biblical literature this central personality was the king, while in stories dealing with the times before kings ruled over Israel, this belief is attached to the persons of kings of other nations. In Genesis we read of Abimelech, king of Gerar, that he took unto himself Sarah, not knowing that she was Abraham's wife. After God had revealed to Abimelech in a dream by night the real state of things, Abimelech said to Abraham:

> What hast thou done unto us ? And what have I offended thee that thou hast brought on me and on my kingdom a great sin ?[20]

After what has been said above we shall understand why Abimelech thought his whole kingdom liable to punishment for a sin that he alone had almost committed. A sin committed by the king is visited on his whole kingdom.

The story of Moses who held up his hands to assure the victory of Israel over Amalek[21] was many times expounded both by Jewish and by Christian theology in a lofty spiritual sense. But the text in itself will leave us little if any doubt as to the original meaning of the story:

> And it came to pass, when Moses held up his hand that Israel prevailed : and when he let down his hand, Amalek prevailed. But Moses' hands were heavy ; and they took a stone, and put it under him, and he sat thereon; and Aaron and Hur stayed up his hands the one on the one side and the other on the other side ; and his hands were steady until the going down of the sun. And Joshua discomfited Amalek and his people with the edge of the sword.[22]

What we have here is a clear instance of the direct sympathy between the leader and his people. When the leader holds up his hands, his people gain the upper hand in the struggle; when his hands tire and sink down, his people too tire and are beaten—hence the very physical help Aaron and Hur had to extend to Moses in holding up his hands.[23]

If this last example was a very exceptional instance of direct sympathetic connection between the leader and his people, the next two examples will again show how the actions of the king involved the welfare of his whole people through the medium of natural forces. The Gibeonites had had a " safe conduct " sworn to them by the Children of Israel, but King Saul, giving no heed to this ancient oath, slew a great number of Gibeonites. This perjury caused a famine lasting three years, until seven of the surviving sons of Saul were handed over by David to the Gibeonites that they might avenge their kinsmen's death.[24] On the other hand, when David numbered Israel and

Judah, this sin on the part of the king cost seventy thousand of his people their lives; this was the number of the victims of the pestilence that broke out as a consequence of David's sin.[25]

Before the rabbinic material is considered, brief evidence must be given that the belief in the king's influence on nature takes an important place also in the writings of the prophets and in the Psalms. The righteous rule of the " rod that shall come forth out of the stem of Jesse " will, according to Isaiah, have a wondrous effect also on the animal kingdom:

> The wolf shall dwell with the lamb, and the leopard shall lie down with the kid; and the calf and the young lion and fatling together; and a little child shall lead them.[26]

Similarly Joel:

> And it shall come to pass in that day that the mountains shall drop down new wine, and the hills shall flow with milk, and all the rivers of Judah shall flow with waters and a fountain shall come forth of the house of the Lord, and shall water the valley of Shittim.[27]

Again in Psalm 72 we have a more detailed description of the beneficial effects of the rule of the righteous king: It will be like rain that comes down upon the mown grass, and as showers that water the earth, and the good people flourish under him. His dominion shall expand. He will conquer all his enemies. " There shall be plenty of corn in the earth upon the top of the mountains (almost unbelievable in Palestine where the tops of the mountains are mostly bare of any soil), the fruit thereof shall rustle like Lebanon and they of the city shall flourish like grass of the earth."[28]

It will be of some interest to compare this passage with a few lines from the *Odyssey*, which show that exactly the same ideas as to the responsibility of the king for the food-supply prevailed in Homeric Greece. "Thy fame, O lady," said the disguised Odysseus to his wife, "shall reach the wide heavens, like that of some blameless king who, in the fear of god ruling over men many and stalwart, upholds the right, and black earth bears wheat and barley, the trees are laden with fruit, the flocks bear young without fail, the sea produces fish, by reason of good government, and the people prosper under him."[29]

III

Let us see now what talmudic literature has to say on this subject. Concerning the episode of David, the Gibeonites and the sons of Saul, rabbinic sources have it that "in the first year (of the famine) David began to admonish his generation at the time of the pilgrimage (when the Israelites gathered together in Jerusalem) and said to them, Perchance there are among you people who serve foreign gods, for the heavens are not shut up from giving dew and rain but on account of this sin. They went out and searched and did not find. The second year he said to them, Perchance there are among you people who commit incest, for the heavens are not shut up but on account of this sin. They went out and searched and did not find. The third year he said unto them, Perchance there are among you people who shed blood, or who promise in public to give alms and do not keep their promise, or who withhold the tithes, for the rains are not kept back but on account of these sins. They went out and searched and did not find. Thereupon David said, The cause must lie in no-one but myself. So he began to ask the *Urim w'Tummim* (the oracle) 'and the Lord answered, It is for Saul and for his bloody house,'[30] for Saul that you did not show grace to him and he was not mourned for as he should have been . . . and for his bloody house, because he slew the Gibeonites.''[31]

What should especially be noted in this legend is that the king, when confronted with the phenomenon of drought, begins to investigate what sin might be the cause of it. The same notion occurs also in the following Indian story:

The god did not rain in the kingdom of Kalinga, and a famine arose, and fear of pestilence through lack of food. The people from all the kingdom gathered together, and came to the capital, and made an outcry at the king's gate. The king standing by the window heard the noise and inquired the cause. They told him why and entreated him, " Make the god to rain, O Great King! " The king asked, " What did the ancient kings do when the god did not rain ? "—" They gave alms," was the reply, " they kept the Sabbath, made vows of virtue, and retiring to the royal chamber lay seven days on a grass mat. Then the god rained." The king did so, but still there was no rain. Then they said, " Dhananjaya, king of the Kurus, observes the Law of the Kurus; therefore in his kingdom the god rains every fortnight or ten days.

That is the power of the king's merit." So the king of Kalinga bade them bring home written on a plate of gold the Law of the Kurus which Dhananjaya observed. Now the law of the Kurus consisted of five commandments : " thou shalt not kill ; thou shalt not steal ; thou shalt not commit adultery ; thou shalt not lie ; thou shalt not drink intoxicants."[32] These not only the king observed faithfully, but his mother, his chief queen, his younger brother, the viceroy, the chaplain, the brahman, the land-surveyor, the councillor, the chief merchant, the collector of taxes, the prime minister, the porter, the courtesan. One and all however disclaimed faithful observance of the law. Each one alleged some petty and unintentional breach which weighed on his mind. . . . " The king abiding in the Kuru law fulfilled the five commandments. Then the god rained in the whole kingdom of Kalinga."[33]

A particularly interesting similarity in the stories about David and about the king of Kalinga consists in the idea that the rains are shut off even in consequence of sins committed by the king unknowingly. It is difficult to understand why the deity should punish the people so severely for a sin of which the king is not even aware, and which is discovered only after the most painstaking search. But if it is, or rather originally was, the sin itself that by its very occurrence brought about the dread consequence directly and without any higher intervention, then we can well understand that regarding the automatic effect there is no difference whatsoever between a sin perpetrated purposely and a sin committed unwittingly. Thus it is in this more original belief in the direct connection between sin and punishment that we have to look for the sources of that mental attitude which deduces from every misfortune that some sin or other, whether intentional or not, must previously have been committed.

What appears in the form of stories and legends in Indian and rabbinic literature and elsewhere was in the life of ancient Mesopotamia dire reality. In the Sumero-Accadian world the king was continually and anxiously inquiring about hidden sins and had often to perform expiatory rites.[34] The ancient Babylonians were continually haunted by the fear of offending their gods, and as in the other instances they too became conscious of having committed a sin only as a conclusion drawn from the fact that some misfortune had overtaken them and had been interpreted as a punishment sent by an offended god.[35]

IV

It is now time to pass on to another type of rabbinic legends, in which the persons who rule over nature are not patriarchs and kings of yore but wise and pious men who had lived but a generation or two before the time of those who told the legends, or even were their contemporaries. The influence of these men over the weather was conceived in the following way. On the strength of their outstanding piety, or even of one single but extremely meritorious deed, they may turn to God who will in no case fail to fulfil their request. This, indeed, is a high religious idea, and were it not for the fact that the benefits asked for concern almost exclusively the weather, one would hardly recognize beneath it the ancient substratum of the sympathy between man and nature.

Of the men having power over the weather let us begin with the type called "whisperers." Their power over nature, as over various ills, did not emanate from their moral qualities but from their technical knowledge, as it were, of the appropriate charms to be whispered. They knew certain magical formulae which were regarded as potent charms. The whispered formulae consisted mostly of quotations from the Bible or of unintelligible magic words, to establish the original meaning of which is a task as yet to be solved by comparative folklore. Such whispered charms were used to cure wounds,[36] to cure sore eyes,[37] or to help a person in whose throat something has got stuck,[38] and the like. The whispering was done directly into the ear of the sick person.[39] Such whisperings were used also to ward off snakes and scorpions,[40] and frequently they were connected with oil-magic.[41] As to the influence of these whisperers over nature, we have a statement from Rabbi Ammi. He said:

> If you see a generation over whom the heavens are rust-coloured like copper so that neither dew nor rain falls, it is because that generation is wanting in whisperers. What then is their remedy? Let them go to someone who knows how to whisper. . . .[42]

Another class of men, to whom much greater influence was attributed, was that of the "pious men of the generation," who would succeed even where the "whisperer" failed:

But if he has whispered and was not answered, what is his remedy? Let him go to the most pious man of that generation that he may intercede abundantly for him. . . .[43]

Yet a third class consisted of "men of faith," while those who succeeded in attaining a more lasting influence over Judaism than any of the preceding were the "Righteous," the "Tzaddiqim." According to a saying recorded in the name of Rabbi Ammi: "Rain falls only for the sake of men of faith."[44]

The most famous of all the meritorious men who could produce rain was Honi Hame'aggel, that is, Honi the Circle-Drawer. The following story tells of the reason for his name:

It happened that the people said to Honi the Circle-Drawer, "Pray for rain to fall." He replied, "Go and bring in the ovens (on which you have roasted) the paschal offerings so that they do not dissolve (being of clay)." He prayed but no rain fell. What did he do? He drew a circle and stood within it and exclaimed: "Master of the Universe! Thy children have turned to me for that I am like a son of the house before you. I swear by thy great name that I will not move from here until thou hast mercy upon thy children." Rain then began to drip, and thereupon he exclaimed: "It is not for this that I have prayed, but for rain [to fill] cisterns, ditches and caves." The rain then began to come down with great force, and thereupon he exclaimed: "It is not for this that I have prayed, but for rain of benevolence, blessing and bounty." Rain then fell as it should until the Israelites in Jerusalem were compelled to go up (for shelter) to the Temple Mount because of the rain. They came and said to him: "In the same way as you have prayed [for the rains] to fall, pray for the rain to cease." He replied: "Go and see if the stone of the claimants (this was a high stone from which lost and found property was announced[45]) has been washed away."

Thereupon Shimeon ben Shetah[46] sent to him saying : " Were it not that you are Honi, I would have placed you under the ban, but what can I do unto you who importune God and He accedes to your request as a son that importunes his father and he accedes to his request. . . .[47]

It is interesting to note that not only the simple folk but also the sages, the spiritual and religious leaders of the people, firmly believed in the powers of Honi. The " Men of the Hall of Hewn Stones," that is, the Sanhedrin, the great council that met in the Hall of Hewn Stones, even sent to him the following acknowledgment:

You have decreed [on earth] below, and the Holy One blessed be He fulfils your word [in heaven] above.[48]

The power to influence the rains passed down in inheritance, as it were, from Honi to his grandchildren.

Abba Hilkiya was a grandson of Honi the Circle-Drawer, and whenever the world was in need of rain the Rabbis sent a message to him and he prayed and rain fell.[49]

Another grandchild of Honi the Circle-Drawer was Hanan-who-hid-himself. He was the son of the daughter of Honi. We have already seen how school-children would be sent to him with a request for rain and how he used to transmit their innocent pleading to God.[50] Of this Hanan also Josephus reports that he prayed to God to give rain, and not without success. Josephus calls him Onias, and tells of him that he " hid himself because he saw that the unrest in his country would last a great while."[51] This is reported in rabbinic sources of a third grandson of Honi, also called Honi Hame'aggel: he hid himself in a cave and slept there for seventy years.[52]

Very interesting is the idea that when a pious man requests something it will unfailingly be fulfilled, but the fulfilment of his wish is a " troubling of heaven." So it is related of Rabha that King Sapor once wanted to punish him, but Iphra Hormuz, the mother of the king, said to her son:

Do not interfere with the Jews, because whatever they ask of their god he grants them. The king asked her, " For example ? " " They pray and rains fall," [she replied]. He retorted, " That must have been because it was the season for rain ; let them pray now, in the Tammuz cycle for rain." She sent a message to Rabha : " Concentrate now your mind and pray for rain." He prayed but no rain fell. He then exclaimed : "Master of the Universe ! 'O God we have heard with our ears, our fathers have told us, a work thou didst in their days, in the days of old.'[53] But as for us, we have not seen it with our eyes." Whereupon there followed such a heavy fall of rain that the gutters of Mahuza[54] emptied their waters into the Tigris. Rabha's father then appeared unto him in a dream and said to him : "Is there anyone who troubles Heaven so much ? Change your [sleeping] place." He changed his place and next morning he discovered that his bed had been cut with knives.[55]

Another story tells of the son of Rabbi Yose of Yoqereth :

Once Rabbi Yose had day-labourers [working] in the field. Night set in and no food was brought to them and they said to his son : " We are hungry." Now they were resting under a fig-tree and he exclaimed : " Fig-tree, fig-tree, bring forth thy fruit that my father's labourers may eat." It brought forth fruit and they ate. Meanwhile the father came and said to them : " Do not bear a grievance against me ; the reason for my delay is that I have been occupied up till now on an errand of charity." The labourers replied : "May God satisfy you even as your son has satisfied us." Whereupon he asked : "Whence ?" And they told him what had happened. Thereupon he said to his son : "My son, you have troubled your creator to cause the fig-tree to bring forth its fruits before its time, may you too be taken hence before your time."

And so it happened.[56]

In biblical times the usual procedure to avert drought or any other great evil was to pray and to fast. Fasting was the habitual expression of repentance and the means of arousing the compassion of God.[57] The same usage prevails also among other peoples.[58] In rabbinic literature too we find the causal connection between sins and drought on the one hand, and between repentance and rain on the other. The feeling of repentance is usually expressed by fasting and by prayers performed on behalf of the community by a pious man. Rabbi Shemuel bar Nahmani, for instance, said:

> When Israel commits sins and bad actions, the rains become shut up. Then they bring themselves an old man like Rabbi Yose the Galilean, and he intercedes on their behalf and the rains fall.[59]

Such a power was ascribed to a sage who belonged to the circle of Rabbi Jehuda the Patriarch, and of whom several sayings and explanations of Bible-verses are preserved in the Babylonian and the Palestinian Talmuds. "Rabbi [Jehuda the Patriarch] proclaimed a fast, and Rabbi Hiyya and his sons were bidden to descend (to the reading desk to pray). As he (Rabbi

Hiyya) exclaimed, 'He causes the wind to blow,' a wind blew. He proceeded, 'He causes the rain to descend,' whereat the rain descended. When he was about to say, 'He quickeneth the dead' (this is the sequel of the prayer), the universe trembled."[60]

It often happens that the fasting and the prayer is of no avail, and then the pious man, confident in his strength, admonishes and rebukes heaven, or even God himself.

Rabbi Hama bar Hanina ordained a fast, but no rain fell. People said to him, "When Rabbi Joshua ben Levi ordained a fast, rain did fall." He replied, "I am I, and he is the son of Levi (that is, he is greater). Go and ask him that he may come (and pray for us). And let us concentrate on our prayer, perhaps the whole community will be contrite in heart and rain will fall." They prayed and no rain fell. He then asked them: "Are you content that rain should fall on our account?" They replied, "Yes." He then exclaimed, "Heaven, heaven, cover thy face (with clouds)." But it did not cover (its face). He then added: "How brazen is the face of heaven!" It then became covered and rain fell.

Levi ordained a fast but no rain fell. He thereupon exclaimed, "Master of the Universe! Thou didst go up and take thy seat on high and hast no mercy upon thy children." Rain fell, but he became lame. . . .

Rabbi Hiyya ben Luliani, overhearing the clouds saying to one another, "Come, let us take water to Ammon and Moab," exclaimed: "Master of the Universe! When thou wast about to give the law to thy people Israel, thou didst offer it about amongst all the nations of the world, but they would not accept it, and now thou wouldst give them rain? Let them (the clouds) empty their waters here!" And they emptied their waters on the spot.[61]

Once it happened that (the inhabitants of Sepphoris) were compelled to call a fast, but no rain fell. (At the same time)

Rabbi Joshua ordered a fast in the south and rain fell; (whereupon) the Sepphoreans said, "Rabbi Joshua ben Levi brought rain to the southerners and Rabbi Hanina held back the rain from the Sepphoreans." Another time they were compelled to make (a fast). (Rabbi Hanina) sent and invited Rabbi Joshua ben Levi, saying to him, "Let the master take care and come out with us (before the synagogue) to fast. They both went out to fast but no rain fell. (Whereupon Rabbi Joshua) entered (the synagogue) and said before them: "Not Rabbi Joshua ben Levi brings down rain for the southerners and not Rabbi Hanina withholds rain from the Sepphoreans; but the southerners, their hearts are soft, they hear the words of the Teaching (that is, the admonition) and they humble themselves, whereas the Sepphoreans, their hearts are hard, they hear the words of the Teaching but do not humble themselves." When he returned (to the place before the synagogue where the fasting was held) and lifted up his eyes and saw that the air is clear (that is, there are no clouds), he said: "After all (these prayers) still so (clear is the air)!" Whereupon immediately rain fell. And he made a vow not do so again, saying (to himself), "Who am I to tell the Creditor that He should not collect His debt (that is, the punishment)!"[62]

In a previous chapter it was pointed out that according to ancient Hebrew belief, both biblical and rabbinic, fornication was the original sin, which caused the deluge, storms, lack of rain and as a consequence famine, as well as all kinds of other natural calamities.[63] This belief was supplemented by the concept that a person who prevents fornication thereby acquires such a great merit as to be able to bring down rain by his prayer. There are quite a number of stories or legends to this effect in the Palestinian Talmud, of which the following is an example:

Rabbi Abbahu saw in a dream that a fivefold sinner (in the original a Greek form, πεντακακός, is used) should pray and then rain would fall. (So it happened) and rain fell. (Thereupon) Rabbi Abbahu sent for him and let him be brought to him. He said to him : " What is your work ? " He (the fivefold sinner) said to him : " Five sins I commit every day. I lease prostitutes, decorate the theatre, carry their garments to the bath, clap hands and dance before them, and beat the drums before them." (Rabbi Abbahu) said to him : " And what good deed did you do ? " He said to him : " Once when I was busy decorating the theatre, a woman came there and remained standing behind a column and wept. I asked her, What (is the matter) with you ? And she said to me, ' My husband has fallen into captivity and I want to prostitute myself and ransom him (with my earnings).' And I sold my bed and my blanket and gave her the money and said to her, Here, ransom your husband and do not sin ! " (Rabbi Abbahu when he heard his story) said to him : " Worthy are you to pray and to be answered ! "[64]

The moral tone of this story is unmistakable.

V

According to Rabbi Johanan the study of the Torah, the Law, for its own sake was such a great merit as to " protect the whole world."[65] According to Rabbi Halbo in the name of Rabh Huna, " the words of every man in whom there is the fear of heaven are heard, as it is written, ' Let us hear the conclusion of the whole matter: Fear God and keep his commandments : for this is the whole of man.'[66] What do the words ' for this is the whole of man ' mean ? Rabbi Eleazar said :

The Holy One blessed be He said : The whole world was

created for nothing but for this (namely, the fear of God). Rabbi Abba bar Kahana said : This (the fear of God) counterbalances the whole of the world.[67]

When one compares these sayings with the function of the " whisperers " referred to earlier, one cannot fail to notice how the religious-moral element gains here the upper hand over the earlier " magical " method of influencing the weather. Not only that the God-fearing, pious man does not need to perform any specific act to have his wish realized, but his influence is no longer confined to the bringing about of relief in a situation of special need, and his voice is heard whenever he raises it.

Let us consider here the striking parallel to this trend of development which is to be found in Moslem religious thought. In the pagan Arab world the following magical ceremony served to bring about the fall of rain in times of drought. Boughs of *Sala*ʻ-trees (*saelanthus*) and ʻ*Ushar*-trees were bound to the tails of oxen. The branches then were set on fire and the oxen were driven, dragging the burning branches after them, to the top of a mountain and were thrown down from there.[68] This procedure, called " *nār alistisqā*'," fire of watering,[69] was superseded in the days of the Islam by the " *salāt al-istisqā*'," the prayer of watering, that is, the prayer for rain.[70] And just as in talmudic Judaism the performance of the prayer by the pious and righteous men was believed to be always crowned with success, so Islam ascribed the same success to outstanding figures in its early history. Almutawakkil inscribed on a memorial coin a poem which told about the family of Hashim that "through their merit rain is given to the earth after it had been withheld for a long time by God."[71] Again, Ibn al-Rūmī says in a *qasida* dedicated to the Caliph Al-Mu'tadid (279-289 H): "Your forefather, Al-'Abbās, is the one whose name did not fail if used in the hour of need to obtain rain; he burst the clouds by intensive prayer and the flashings of the water-giving lightnings did his will."[72] Of 'Omar it is recorded that in times of drought he said in his "*istisqā*'": "O Allah! We used in our requests to appeal to the Prophet, and you gave us rain; to-day we appeal to the uncle of the Prophet (Al-'Abbās), so give us rain!" And his request was granted.[73] In later days too the prayers for rain contained an appeal to contemporary holy men.[74]

To return to Judaism, the same sort of development impresses itself upon us when we follow up another line of thought. We have seen in the course of a previous chapter that the blessings of the material world, such as rain, abundant crops, fruit, etc., were attributed to the merit of certain ritual functions in the Temple. This idea—that the natural forces in the world function in a manner beneficial to man only as a reward for certain merits—also developed from a physical-ritual conception in a spiritual-moral direction. The "merit" becomes attached to a great variety of subjects, both concrete and abstract, until finally it settles on the person of the "Righteous," that is on men who are meritorious on account of their outstanding moral qualities.[75]

We read, for instance, the following sentence handed down by Rabbi Berekhya and Rabbi Halbo Papa, in the name of Rabbi Eleazar:

> Sometimes it happens that the rains fall by the merit of one man, by the merit of one grass, by the merit of one field. . . .[76]

The merit of the field to bring down rain is stressed also by Rabbi Simon.[77] Again, another saying has it:

> By the merit of three things the rains fall : by the merit of the earth ; by the merit of the mercy ; and by the merit of the sufferings.[78]

The same idea in a general but negative form was expressed by Rabbi Shimeon ben Yohai with the aid of a simile:

> Just as the mountains press down the waters of the Deep that they should not rise and flood the world, even so charity (in Hebrew : *tz'daqah*) presses down the severe judgment (of God) and the divine retribution that they should not come upon the world.[79]

Also the merit of two commandments alone, if kept by Israel, suffices to secure them the fall of rain: They are the Sabbath and the circumcision.[80]

The Fathers of Israel were the first men whose merits secured lasting benefits to coming generations.

> Rabbi Jacob of Kfar Hanan said in the name of Rabbi Shimeon ben Laqish : (God said to Israel) : In the hour when Abraham, your father, fulfilled my will,[81] I swore unto him that I shall not remove the dew from his sons forever. . . .[82]

Abraham received hospitably the angels,[83] and how did the Holy One blessed be He pay it back to his sons? The manna descended for them and the well[84] rose up for them, and the quails were found for them,[85] and the Clouds of Glory surrounded them, and the Column of Clouds travelled before them. . . .[86] In a fine simile we are given to understand how the merits of Abraham carried, as it were, all the generations:

> Rabbi Abba bar Kahana said: It is customary in the world that if a man has a pair of double-beams, where does he put them? Is it not (that he puts them) in the middle of the hall, in order that they should carry the crossbeams (of the roof) which are both in front of them and behind them? Thus why did the Holy One blessed be He create Abraham in the middle of the generations? In order that he should carry the generations (which were) before him and (those which came) after him. . . .[87]

And just as in time the merit of Abraham reached from the beginning to the end, so in space it reached to the very ends of the world:

> Rabbi Hanina said: Even the ships which were sailing in the sea were saved (from shipwreck only) by the merits of Abraham.[88]

Notwithstanding this, it is the actual presence of the Righteous One which secures real blessings. "Our fathers came to the country (that is, to Palestine) and blessing came through them,"[89] says a midrashic passage. And again:

> Wherever the Righteous go, blessing comes (through them). Isaac descended to Gerar, blessing came to Gerar . . . Jacob descended to Laban, blessing descended through him . . . Joseph descended to Potiphar, blessing came through him . . . Jacob descended to Pharaoh, blessing descended through

him, as it is written, "and Jacob blessed Pharaoh."[90] What did he bless him with? That the years of hunger ceased. . . .[91]

Also according to Rabbi Yose ben Hanina: the hunger in Egypt which, according to the dream of Pharaoh, should have lasted seven years,[92] lasted only two years for when Jacob descended to Egypt the hunger ceased.[93] Jacob and Joseph were both men of blessing to an equal extent:

> This one, the house of his father-in-law (Laban) became blessed for him; and that one, the house of his father-in-law (Potiphera) became blessed for him. . . . This one stopped the hunger, and that one stopped the hunger; this one satisfied (with food), and that one satisfied (with food). . . .[94]

Jacob's presence caused a wonderful multiplication of the water in the house of Laban. "You know," Laban later reminded his townsmen, "that we were hard pressed for water, and as soon as this Righteous One came, the waters became blessed."[95] And how did this miracle happen? When Jacob rolled the stone from the well's mouth,[96] "the well rose and poured forth water outside (its brim) and the shepherds saw it and wondered."[97] All the twenty years Jacob spent with Laban, the waters of the well poured forth in abundance, but on the day that Jacob fled from Laban, the miracle ceased and the waters never rose again.[98]

In these passages the expression rendered by the words "through him" ("the blessing came through him," etc.) is in the original Hebrew "*l'raglo*," having the primary meaning of "by his foot" ("the blessing came by his foot"). The same expression is used already in Genesis. Jacob said to Laban: "The Lord hath blessed thee through me,"[99] *l'ragli*, verbatim "by my foot." To this passage the midrash adds:

> There is a man's foot that blesses the house, and there is a man's foot that ruins the house. And the foot of Jacob blessed. . . .[100]

A story similar to that of Jacob in the house of Laban is told in Mohammedan tradition of Abraham. Ibrahim dug a well in Saba', but the inhabitants of the locality molested him so much that he had to go away, whereupon the waters of the well dried up. Then the people of the place begged Ibrahim to return to them.[101] The fathers were a source of blessing even after their death. When Joseph died, the Egyptians "made him a metal coffin and placed it in the River Nile in order that its waters should become blessed."[102]

The belief in the blessing that emanates from the Righteous remained living in traditional Judaism down to modern times. To give only one single example, in the writings of Nahman of Bratzlav, a famous Hassidic rabbi of the eighteenth century, we find the following passage:

> Anyone in whose house the Tzaddiq (that is, the Righteous One; but here used in the specific sense of a rabbi of the Hassidim) sojourns as a guest, becomes blessed with sons.[103]

That is, the Tzaddiq has here the role that was fulfilled by the Ark according to early Jewish legend.

The merit of the Righteous assumes ever more superhuman dimensions:

> Rabha, or, according to others, Rabbi Johanan, said: Were it not for Moses and Aaron, the world could not exist.[104]

The same is stated also of contemporaneous sages:

> Rabbi Jehuda said in the name of Rabh: Every day a heavenly voice comes out from Mount Horeb (that is, Mount Sinai) and says, The whole world receives nourishment for the sake of my son Hanina [ben Dosa]. . . .[105] . . . Rabbi Eleazar said: Even for the sake of a single righteous man this world would have been created. . . Rabbi Hiyya bar Abba said in the name of Rabbi Joshua: Even for the sake of a single righteous man does the world endure.[106]

"The righteous is an everlasting foundation,"[107] is said in the Book of Proverbs. The Hebrew original, "*tzaddiq y'sod 'olam*," can equally be rendered "the righteous is the foundation of the world," and it is on this sense of the passage that Rabbi Ele'azar ben Shamua' (lived about the middle of the second century C.E.) bases his saying that the world stands "on one pillar and *tzaddiq*, the righteous one, is his name."[108] Such a righteous one was Jacob who was the "fundament and foundation of the world."[109] According to Rabbi Eleazar ben Rabbi Shimeon, who lived a generation later than his namesake ben Shamua' (at the end of the second century C.E.), "the world was created for the sake of the righteous, for them it receives blessings, and as long as there are righteous men in the world, there is blessing in the world; once the righteous departed from the world, the blessing departed from the world."[110] In this connection should be quoted also the following passage which is often repeated in talmudic sources:

The world was created with ten pronouncements (the word " said " is ten times repeated in Genesis 1 [111]). What does this teach us ? It could have been created with one pronouncement (but it was created with ten), in order to increase the punishment of the wicked who ruin the world which was created with ten pronouncements, and to increase the reward of the righteous who preserve the world which was created with ten pronouncements.[112]

A righteous man may also be one of the Gentiles.

Rabbi Hanan said : In the cities of the sea sins are committed the like of which was not even in the generation of the deluge . . . so they would deserve extermination. And by what merit do they exist ? By the merit of one Gentile (another version has : one proselyte) whom the Holy One blessed be He receives from them every year.[113]

The righteous one also takes upon himself the punishment of his generation. The righteous one suffers and his generation is redeemed from divine retribution.

Our Master (that is, Rabbi Jehuda the Patriarch) suffered for thirty years. . . . And in all those thirty years no woman died in childbirth in the land of Israel, nor did a woman miscarry in the land of Israel. . . .

When he was cured:

Rabbi Hiyya said : Woe to you women in childbirth in the land of Israel, woe to you pregnant women in the land of Israel! . . .[114]

Again, Shemuel, or, according to others, Rabbi Eleazar, said:

The whole world is nourished for the merit of the righteous, but they themselves are not nourished even by their own merit. . . .

To this Rabbi Jehuda in the name of Rabh added by way of illustration :

> Every day a heavenly voice comes out from Mount Horeb (Sinai) and says : The whole world is nourished for the sake of my son Hanina, and my son Hanina contents himself with one small measure of carobs from one Friday evening to the next.[115]

In a previous chapter an account was given of the belief that the mere existence of the Temple secured the orderly functioning of nature and prevented the occurrence of natural calamities.[116] The same function, as we have just seen, was ascribed also to the Righteous and the Pious. And it is also owing to this belief that the rainbow was supposed to be absent during the lifetime of a truly righteous man. In Genesis it is related that God made a covenant with Noah, saying: "I do set my bow in the cloud and it shall be for a token of a covenant between me and the earth. And it shall come to pass when I bring clouds over the earth that the bow shall be seen in the clouds. And I will remember my covenant . . . and the waters shall no more become a flood to destroy all flesh."[117] According to talmudic conception, whenever the rainbow appears in the sky, it is a sign that the sins of the generation should by rights be punished with a new flood—were it not for the oath of God not to bring a second deluge on the earth. Thus it happens that no rainbow appears in the days of a pious generation, when there is no need of reminding God of his covenant. Such pious generations were those of

King Hezekiah and of the Men of the Great Council, in whose days the rainbow was absent.[118]

If a generation or a community was sinful, as ordinary generations or communities would be, there had to be in it at least one single pious man by whose merits the others too were saved from destruction. If the piety of this man was very great, the rainbow did not appear in his lifetime, since his mere existence sufficed to ward off destruction from the world. Such an exceedingly pious man was Rabbi Shimeon ben Yohai, in whose days the rainbow never appeared in the clouds.[119] The sages once entered to him and said to him:

> Why is it that the rainbow never appeared in your days? He said to them: What else is (the rainbow) but (a sign) of punishment? I am worthy to withhold the punishment. . . . One of the sages present, on hearing this, rose up and said: "I set my bow in the clouds,"[120] this is Rabbi Shimeon ben Yohai, who is the sign of the world. . . .[121]

The appearance of the rainbow thus became a criterion of the real piety of an outstanding man. If the rainbow appeared in his days—he was not a "*tzaddiq gamur*," a perfectly righteous man, but he was regarded as such if the rainbow did not appear as long as he lived. Thus it is related of Rabbi Joshua ben Levi, who lived some generations after Rabbi Shimeon ben Yohai, that "Elijah of blessed memory was studying with him the Law, and they were occupied in the teachings of Rabbi Shimeon ben Yohai. Rabbi Joshua ben Levi had difficulties concerning a decision. Elijah said to him: Do you want to ask it of Rabbi Shimeon ben Yohai ? Come, and I shall raise him (from the dead) for you. At once they went and Elijah called Rabbi Shimeon ben Yohai. At once he answered him. (Elijah) said to him: Rabbi Joshua ben Levi has come to ask you a decision. And (Shimeon ben Yohai) did not want (to answer him). (Whereupon) Elijah said to him: Rabbi Joshua ben Levi is worthy of seeing you. He is a righteous man. (Rabbi Shimeon ben Yohai) said: Were he righteous, the rainbow would not have appeared in his days."[122]

VI

Reference has already been made in this book to the distinct messianic colouring of the ancient Near Eastern concept of the king's beneficial influence on his people's welfare.[123] It has been shown too that in biblical literature, in the Prophets and the Psalms, the same concept prevails: the days of the Messiah, the future king, are characterized not only by his righteousness which secures social justice and happiness for his people, but also—or, one may say, mainly—by the "messianic peace" in the animal kingdom and the wondrous fertility of all the creatures and the plants. These motives are very amply elaborated in rabbinic literature, often showing in their details surprising correspondence to the ancient Near Eastern ideas on the subject. Their general tenor, though, is different. While in the ancient Near Eastern texts *living* kings are flatteringly characterized as bringing " messianic " prosperity to their country and people, the rabbinic material assigns the blissful state only to the "golden age" of a far-away past, and to the eschatological era of the " days to come," whereas the present is full of suffering and privations caused by the sins of man.

Let us begin our survey of the rabbinic statements with a quotation from Exodus Rabba:

> We find that the Holy One blessed be He will renew ten things in the days to come. . . . One : he will light up the world . . . even a sick man—the Holy One blessed be He will command the sun to cure him. . . . Two : He will cause to come forth living water from Jerusalem and cure with it all the sick. . . . Three : He will cause the trees to yield fruit every month and people will eat them and be cured. . . . Four : all the ruined cities will be rebuilt and there will be no desolate place in the world. . . . Five : He will build up Jerusalem in sapphire stones . . . and those stones will shine like unto the sun and the idolators will come and see the honour of Israel. . . . Six : the cow and the bear will feed together. . . .[124] Seven : He will bring all the beasts and all the birds and all the creeping things, and will make a covenant between them and Israel. . . . Eight : there will be no weeping and wailing in the world. . . . Nine : there will be no more death in the world. . . . Ten : there will be no more sigh, no more groan and no more sorrow, but everybody will be rejoicing. . . .[125]

Another source speaks not of ten things but of no fewer than " twenty-four good traits [which] were in the world and were put to naught by the sins, and at the end of the days the Holy One blessed be He will restore them to Israel." They are: Man's likeness to God; his stature (which was diminished); the garden of Eden; the tree of life; the heroism;

longevity; great number of children; the peace; the holy language (Hebrew); richess; the fruits; the manna; the well (which accompanied Israel in the wilderness); the pillar of fire; the pillar of smoke; the Tetragrammaton (the Ineffable Name); the rejoicing; the spring of Gihon; the Synhedrion; the kingship of David's house; the office of the High Priest; the Sanctuary; and the Holy Spirit.[126]

On some of these future blessings the sages have dwelt with special interest:

Rabbi Hiyya b. Joseph said: There will be a time when the land of Israel will produce baked cakes of the purest quality and silk [or woollen] garments. . . .[127]

Our rabbis taught: " There will be a rich cornfield upon the top of the mountains."[128] [From this] it was inferred that there will be a time when wheat will rise as high as a palm-tree and will grow on the top of the mountains. But in case you should think that there will be trouble in reaping it, it was specifically said in Scripture, " Its fruit shall rustle like Lebanon."[129] The Holy One blessed be He will bring a wind from his treasure houses which He will cause to blow upon it. This will loosen its fine flour and a man will walk out into the field and take a mere handful and, out of it, will [have sufficient provision for] his own, and his household's maintenance.

" With the kidney-fat of wheat."[130] [From this] it was inferred that there will be a time when a grain of wheat will be as large as the two kidneys of a big bull. . . .

" And of the blood of the grape thou drankest foaming wine."[131] It was inferred: The world to come is not like this world. In this world there is the trouble of harvesting and treading [of the grapes], but in the world to come a man will bring one grape on a wagon or a ship, put it in a corner of his house and use its contents as [if it had been] a large wine cask, while its timber (*i.e.* the stalk of the grape) would be used to make fires for cooking (lit.: under the dish).

There will be no grape that will not contain thirty kegs of wine. . . .[132]

Or again:

Each vine in the days of the Messiah will require no less than a whole town to gather its grapes . . . and trees that have never borne fruit will bear fruit. . . .[133]

Every tree and every grass and every wild tree will bear fruit in the days to come.[134]

Rabbi Jehuda said: In this world the crop ripens in six months and the trees bear fruit in twelve months; but in the days to come the crops will ripen in one month and the wild trees will bear fruit every two months. . . . Rabbi Yose said: . . . the crops will ripen in fifteen days and the trees will bear fruit in one month. . . .[135]

The wonderful fertility of the days of the Messiah will extend to man as well as to plant:

R. Gamliel said: In the days to come a woman will bear children every day . . . the trees will yield fruit every day. . . .[136]

The Messiah, whose appearance will bring all these wonderful blessings, was conceived in the talmudic period as scarcely more than an earthly king. This is evident from the concept of the Messiah as the son of David (or Joseph), and even more so from a legend which has it that the Holy One blessed be He wished to make Hezekiah the Messiah and Sennacherib Gog and Magog. But as Hezekiah never sang a song of praise to God, he was found lacking.[137]

Let us now put into parallel columns the features by which the king's beneficent rule is characterized in ancient Near Eastern texts,[138] and which are to mark, according to rabbinic tradition, the days of the Messiah:

THE KING	THE MESSIAH
New Foundations	
Ass. " Maker of Assyria "	Cities rebuilt
Founder of the palace	Jerusalem built in precious stones [139]
Renewer of the temples	The Temple rebuilt
Sustainer of the cult places [140]	The office of the High Priest and David's house restored
Blessing of the Light	
Eg. The days are long	The world is lit up
Bab. " The sun of Babylonia "	The Temple will light up the world [141]
Ass. " The sun of all peoples " [142]	The sun shines sevenfold [143]
	The " righteous " will shine [144]
Blessing of the Waters	
Eg. " Lord of flood." The Nile runs high	Living waters issue from Jerusalem
Ass. Abundant rains Copious inundations	The " Well " and the spring of Gihon appears
Blessing of the Vegetable World	
Eg. Plentiful in grain	Even wild trees bear fruit
Ass. Years of abundance	The land produces ready-baked cakes
The hungry are satisfied	
The corn grows 5 ells high	Wheat high as a palm-tree
	A grain of wheat as large as two kidneys
The spike becomes five-sixths of an ell	Grapes reach enormous size, each yields 30 kegs of wine
The Giparu tree is ever-bearing	Trees yield fruit every two months—every month—every day. Crops ripen every month—every 15 days
Fruit trees yield luxuriant fruit	The vine yields 926 kinds of fruit [145]
Ras Sh. Power over the crops	Amplitude of wheat, wine and oil [146]
Blessing of the Animal Kingdom	
Ass. Cattle multiply greatly	Fishes will multiply, and
Hitt. Cattle, sheep multiply	Mountains will flow of milk and honey [147]
Tel Am. Gives sheep, flock, cattle	

Blessing of Human Progeny	
Ass. Many children born	Many children born
Hitt. People multiply	Women will bear every day
Health	
Ass. The sick become cured	The sick become cured Bodily defects disappear[148] " The healing dew "[149]
Richess	
Ass. The destitute clothed Acceptable prices	The land produces silk (or: woollen) garments
Tel Am. Clothes the poor in byssus Gives silver, gold, richess	Richess
Lawfulness, Security, Happiness	
Ass. No force, no injury, no outrage, no bloodshed; security on the roads Man and women rejoicing	No sigh, no groan, no sorrow, no weeping, no wailing. Longevity (" Tree of Life," no death.) The Synhedrion.[150] Everybody rejoicing. God makes the world joyful[151]
Victory	
Ass. Enemy subjugated[152] " Brought subjection to the four quarters of the world "[154]	Heroism. " Idolators " come and see the honour of Israel.[153] Victory of Israel.[155] Israel's rule over the world[156]
Peace	
Ass. General peace	Peace between men and between animals[157]

The inference is clear: the " materialistic " traits of the rabbinic messianology go back to the very old conception of the magic or divine king, which was a common heritage of the peoples of the ancient Near East.

It is thus far that we can follow at present the course of development which leads from the magician, the priestly, and the divine king—through the whisperer and rain-maker—to the righteous and pious man, whose moral personality shouldered in rabbinic Judaism the responsibility for the welfare of his people, and whose image was projected into the future, there to become merged with the figure of the Messiah.

The very idea, that one single person is responsible for the whole community, emerges from our investigations as a heritage from cruder ages, in which the responsibility was of a physical, or rather a technical kind. With the advance of the ages the ancient idea of the necessity of performing ritual functions for the purpose of influencing nature and thus obtaining from it material benefits, underwent a slow but steady modification. In consequence of the destruction of the Temple the performance of the sacrificial ritual was stopped before it could become obsolete. In Divine Service the place of the sacrifices was taken by the prayer, while in popular imagination the place of the sacrificing priest, who set in motion the working of sympathy in nature, was taken by the "men of faith," the pious and the righteous, whose influence over nature came to be ascribed in an ever-increasing extent to their moral qualities, to their merits, and even to their sufferings. Instead of physical sympathy there thus developed a concept of spiritual and moral sympathy, in which the responding party was no longer nature but God himself.

1 Philostratus, *Life of Apollonius of Tyana*, viii, 6. Loeb Class. Library, p. 281.

2 Pasquale Villari, *Life and Times of Savonarola*, London, 1888, p. 124.

3 L. Wieger, *Histoire des croyances religieuses et des opinions philosophiques en Chine,* Hien-Hien, 1922, p. 64. (The English translation is mine.)

4 Engnell, *Studies*, pp. 13 sq.

5 Breasted, *Eg. Rec.* III. §§ 265, 268, as quoted by S. A. Cook in Robertson-Smith, *Religion of the Semites*, 3rd ed., p. 537.

6 Jastrow, *The Religion of Babylonia and Assyria*, 1898, pp. 374 sq.

7 Strack, *Assurbanipal*, II, p. 152, lines 5 sqq., as quoted by E. R. Goodenough, " Kingship in Early Israel," *Journal of Biblical Literature*, 1929, pp. 174 sq.

8 *Beiträge zur Assyrologie und Semitischen Sprachwissenschaft*, 3, 254, 10 sq., as quoted by Engnell, *Studies*, p. 29.

9 Engnell, *Studies*, pp. 43 sq.

10 Witzel, *Keilinschriftliche Studien* (1–7, Fulda, 1918–30), 5, pp. 52 sqq., as quoted by Engnell, *Studies*, p. 39.

11 Witzel, *op. cit.*, pp. 76 sqq., as quoted, *ib.* p. 40.

12 *Vorderasiatische Bibliothek*, 4, p. 172, as quoted by Engnell, p. 43.

13 *Annals of Ashurbanapal*, ed. R. J. Lau-S. Langdon (Semitic Study Series, 2, Leiden (1903), ll. 45 sq. as quoted by Engnell, p. 44.

14 Dhorme, *La religion assyro-babylonienne*, Paris, 1910, p. 173.

15 Engnell, *Studies*, pp. 44 sq.

16 *Op. cit.*, p. 68.

17 *Op. cit.*, p. 93.

18 The *Klmw* inscription, as quoted by Engnell, *op. cit.*, pp. 94 sq.

19 Virolleaud, *La légende phénicienne de Danel*, Paris, 1936, pp. 91, 121, 145, as quoted by Engnell, *op. cit.*, p. 104.

20 Gen. 20, 9. Cf also Gen. 26, 10, where the same story is told of Abimelech and Rebecca, the wife of Isaac.

21 Ex. 17, 8–13.

22 Ex. 17, 11–13. About the royal prerogatives of Moses, as pointed out by Philo, etc., cf. E. R. Goodenough,

"Kingship in Early Israel," *Journal of Biblical Literature*, 1929, pp. 178 sqq.

23 Less clear is the stretching out of the spear by Joshua which resulted in the capture of Ai, Josh. 8, 18.

24 2. Sam. 21, 1–9.

25 2 Sam. 24, 1–15 ; 1 Chron. 21, 1–14. Cf. C. R. North, "The Religious Aspects of Hebrew Kingship," *Zeitschrift für alttestamentl. Wissenschaft*, 1932, pp. 10 sq.

26 Is. 11, 1, 6.

27 Joel, 4, 18.

28 Ps. 72, 6–9, 16. Cf. E. R. Goodenough, "Kingship in Early Israel," *J.B.L.*, 1929, pp. 199 sqq.

29 Odyssey xix, 108–14.

30 2 Sam. 21, 1.

31 Num. Rab. 8, 4 ; Midrash Shemuel 28 ; B. Yeb. 78b ; Pirqe Rabbi Eliezer, ch. 17 ; Midrash Shoher Tobh, Ps. 17.

32 These are taken from the Abhidhanappadipika, No. 783. Cf. Digha, ii, 172 sqq. Hocart, *Kingship*, p. 23. (Note of Hocart, *Kings and Councillors*, p. 140.)

33 Jataka, ii. 366 sqq., as quoted by Hocart, *Kings and Councillors*, pp. 140 sq.

34 R. Labat, *Le caractère religieux de la royauté assyro-babylonienne,* Paris, 1939 (*Études d'assyriologie,* 2), p. 328, referred to by Engnell, *Studies*, p. 35.

35 Jastrow, *Religion of Babylonia and Assyria*, pp. 313 sqq. ; Zimmern, *Babylonische Busspsalmen*, passim.

36 M. Sanh. 11, 1 ; B. Sanh. 101a ; Y. Sanh. 28b top.

37 Y. Sotah 16d bot. ; Lev. Rab. 9, 153b ; Num. Rab. 9, 201d.

38 Y. Sab. 14d mid. ; Y. ʻAb. Zar. 40d mid ; Y. Ber. 3c bot.

39 Y. Sab. 8b bot.

40 B. Sanh. 101a.

41 Cf. S. Daiches, *Babylonian Oil Magic in the Talmud and in Later Jewish Literature*, London, 1913.

42 B. Taʻan. 8a.

43 B. Taʻan. 8a.

44 B. Ta'an. 8a.
45 Cf. B. Bab. Metz. 28b.
46 C. 80 B.C.
47 M. Ta'an. 3, 8; cf. B. Ta'an. 23a; Y. Ta'an. 66d–67a. Cf. Patai, "The 'Control of Rain,'" *Hebrew Union Coll. Annual*, xiv, p. 282, notes 159 and 160.
48 B. Ta'an. 23a.
49 B. Ta'an. 23a.
50 B. Ta'an. 23b. Cf. p. 161.
51 Josephus, *Ant*. xiv, 2, 1.
52 Y. Ta'an. 66d bot., but cf. B. Ta'an. 23a.
53 Ps. 44, 2.
54 The town where Rabha lived; current editions have "Sepphoris."
55 B. Ta'an. 24b.
56 B. Ta'an. 24a.
57 Judges 20, 26; 1 Sam. 7, 6 sq.; 10 sq.; 1 Kings 21, 27; 2 Chron. 20, 3; Joel 1, 14; 2, 12; Jer. 36, 9; Ezra 8, 21 sq.; Neh. 9, 1; Ps. 35, 13; Zach. 8, 19.
58 Koran 2, 192; 4, 91, 96; 5, 91; 58, 1 sq.; Westermarck, *Moral Ideas*, ii, 315, 361; *Enc. Bibl.* s.v. Fasting (ii, 1508); Hastings, *Dict. of the Bible*, s.v. Fasting.
59 Y. Ber. 9b top.
60 B. Bab. Metz. 85b.
61 B. Ta'an. 25a.
62 Y. Ta'an. 66c bot.
63 Cf. also Patai, *Man and Earth* ii, 225 sqq., 236 sqq., 245 sqq.
64 Y. Ta'an. 64b bot.
65 B. Sanh. 99b.
66 Eccl. 12, 13.
67 B. Ber. 6b.
68 Al-Jauharī, s.v. sl'; cf. Al-wishāh wa-tathqif al-rimāh (Būlāq 1281, p. 80); Muhīt, s.v. I, p. 981b; Al-Damīrī I, p. 187 sq.; cf. also Wellhausen, *Reste*, 157; as quoted by Goldziher, *Muhammedanische Studien*, i, Halle, 1889, pp. 34 sq.

69 Al-Jāhiz, *Kitāb al-heywān*, fol. 245b, as quoted by Goldziher, ib. p. 35.

70 Koran 71, 9–10.

71 Al-Muwasshā, ed. Brünnow, p. 193, 9, as quoted by Goldziher, ib. ii, p. 108.

72 Yatīmat ad-dahr ii, p. 303, as quoted by Goldziher, ib. p. 109.

73 Aġ. xi, p. 81, Tahdīb, p. 332, as quoted by Goldziher, ib. p. 108.

74 Yāqūt, i, p. 418 bot. as quoted by Goldziher, ib. p. 313. In the following (pp. 313 sqq.) Goldziher adduces data to show that the habit prevailed to pray for rain on the graves of many a holy man. This custom is found also in Oriental Jewish communities.

75 The theological significance of the doctrine of merits was exhaustively treated by A. Marmorstein in his book, *The Doctrine of Merits in Old Rabbinical Literature*, London, 1920; we can, therefore, in the following confine ourselves to a few characteristic examples.

76 Y. Ta'an. 66c top.; Lev. Rab. 35, 12.

77 Y. Ta'an. 66c top.

78 Y. Ta'an. 66c mid.

79 Tanhuma Gen. ed. Buber, p. 34.

80 Pesiqta Rabbati 201b; cf. Eccl. Rab. 11, 2.

81 Cf. Gen. 22, 1–19.

82 Y. Ber. 9b top; Y. Ta'an. 63d top.

83 Gen. 18, 1 sqq.

84 According to legend the so-called Well of Miriam accompanied the Children of Israel everywhere during their wanderings in the wilderness, cf. Patai, *Hammayim* (*The Water*), *a Study in Palestinology and Palestinian Folklore* (in Hebrew), Tel-Aviv, 1936, pp. 153 sqq.

85 Cf. Num. 11, 31.

86 Lev. Rab. 34, 8.

87 Gen. Rab. 14, 6, p. 130.

88 Gen. Rab. 39, 11, p. 376.

89 Siphre Deut. 38.

90 Gen. 7, 47.

91 Siphre Deut. 38.
92 Gen. 41, 27.
93 Gen. Rab. 89, 9, p. 1098.
94 Gen. Rab. 84, 6, p. 1008.
95 Gen. Rab. 70, 19, p. 817; cf. Targum Yer. ad Gen. 29, 22.
96 Gen. 29, 10.
97 Pirqe Rabbi Eliezer, ch. 36; cf. Midrash Haggadol, ed. Schechter, p. 457.
98 Targum Yer. ad Gen. 28, 10; 31, 22.
99 Gen. 30, 30.
100 Pirqe Rabbi, Eliezer, ch. 36. In recognizing the true content of the biblical passages speaking about the blessing which is inherent in the person of the "righteous," and in explicitly stating that this blessing spreads from the person of the "righteous" to his surrounding, the talmudic sages have thus anticipated Pedersen by some fifteen hundred years. Cf. Pedersen, *Israel*, Its Life and Culture, I–II (1926), pp. 209 sqq.
101 Cf. *Encyclopedia of the Islam*, s.v. Ibrahim, p. 432.
102 B. Sotah 13a.
103 Nahman of Bratzlav, *Sepher Hammiddoth*, s.v. banim, no. 78, ed. Traklin, Warsaw, p. 30.
104 B. Hul. 89a.
105 B. Ber. 17b; cf. B. Ta'an. 24b; B. Hul. 86b.
106 B. Yoma 38b.
107 Prov. 10, 25.
108 B. Hag. 12b.
109 Gen. Rab. 75, 11, p. 892.
110 Siphre Deut. 38.
111 Cf. also B. Meg. 21b.
112 M. 'Aboth 5, 1; cf. Fragments of Midrash Abqir, ed. by A. Marmorstein, in "*Debir*," Berlin, 1923, p. 120.
113 Gen. Rab. 28, 5, p. 264; Cant. Rab. ad 1, 4; cf. Jellinek, *Beth Hamidrash*, v, p. xlvi; Schürer, *Geschichte des jüdischen Volkes*, 4th ed., iii, 150–88, where the material is collected concerning Jewish proselytizing.

114 Gen. Rab. 96, 5; cf. Gen. Rab. 33, 3, pp. 306 sq.; Y. Kil. 32b mid.; Tanhuma Wayhi, 13.

115 B. Ber. 17b.

116 See p. 121.

117 Gen. 9, 13–15.

118 Gen. Rab. 35, 2, p. 328; Midrash Haggadol, ed. Schechter, p. 173; cf. Patai, "Haqqesheth," in the *Samuel Krauss Jubilee Volume* (in Hebrew), Jerusalem, 1937, pp. 311 sqq., and especially pp. 319 sq., where evidence is adduced to show the existence of this belief among other peoples.

119 Y. Ber. 13d bot.

120 Gen. 9, 13.

121 Midrash Haggadol, ed. Schechter, p. 174.

122 Midrash Shoher Tobh ed. Buber, p. 252; cf. B. Ket. 74b; Gen. Rab. 35, 2, pp. 328–29; Patai, *Haqqesheth*, pp. 320 sq.

123 See p. 176.

124 Is.ii, 7.

125 Ex. Rab., 15, 21.

126 Midrash Haggadol, Genesis, ed. Schechter, p. 126 sq., cf. additional sources, *ib.* in the notes.

127 Cf. B. Shabbat 30 b, in the name of R. Gamliel.

128 Ps. 72, 16.

129 *Ib. ib.*

130 Deut. 32, 14.

131 *Ib. ib.*

132 B. Kethuboth 111b, translated by I. Slotki in *The Babylonian Talmud,* ed. I. Epstein, Soncino Press, London, 1936, vol. ii, pp. 720 sqq. Cf. Siphre Deut. § 317; Midrash Tannaim, pp. 192 sqq.

133 Pirqē Mashiah, Jellinek, *Beth Hamidrash*, iii, 77. Cf. Apoc. Baruch, 29, 5.

134 Ginzberg, "Aggadoth q'tu'oth," *Haggoren*, ix, Berlin, 1929, p. 66; cf. *ib.* pp. 58–59.

135 Yer. Sheqalim 50a, cf. Kethuboth, 112b.

136 B. Shabbat, 30b. Cf. also Midrash Tanhuma, ed. Buber, Introduction, 158; Gen. 7a, J. Klausner, *Die*

messianischen Vorstellungen im Zeitalter der Tannaiten, pp. 108 sqq ; Schechter, *Some Aspects of Rabbinic Theology*, London, 1909, p. 109; A. Jeremias, *Babyl. im NT*, p. 33; Ginzberg, *The Legends of the Jews*, v, 142, and additional sources, *ib.*; G. Foot Moore, *Judaism*, vol. ii, Cambridge, Mass. 1927, pp. 365 sq.; Patai, *Man and Earth*, i, 282 sq.

137 Cf. Ginzberg, *Legends of the Jews*, iv, 271 sq. and the corresponding notes in vol. iv. Cf. B. Synh, 98b, 99a.

138 Cf. pp. 175 sqq.

139 Pirqē Mashiah, Jellinek, *Beth Hamidrash*, iii, 69.

140 Engnell, *Studies*, pp. 42, 192.

141 Pirqē Mashiah, Jellinek, *Beth Hamidrash*, iii, 69.

142 Engnell, *Studies*, p. 183.

143 B. Synh., 91b.

144 "The Wars of King Messiah," Jellinek, *Beth Hamidrash*, vi, 119.

145 Tanhuma, ed. Buber, Introduction, p. 158.

146 Book of Elijah, Jellinek, *Beth Hamidrash*, iii, 66.

147 Pirqē Mashiah, Jellinek, *Beth Hamidrash*, iii, 74.

148 B. Synh., 91b; "The Wars of King Messiah," Jellinek, *Beth Hamidrash*, vi, 119.

149 "The Signs of the Messiah," Jellinek, *Beth Hamidrash*, ii, 59.

150 Cf. Is. 2, 4.

151 Pirqē Mashiah, Jellinek, *Beth Hamidrash*, iii, 70.

152 Cf. also Engnell, *Studies*, pp. 187 sq.

153 Cf. Is. 2, 3.

154 Engnell, *Studies*, 188.

155 Pirqē Mashiah, Jellinek, *Beth Hamidrash*, iii, 69, 70, 71.

156 "The Wars of King Messiah," Jellinek, *Beth Hamidrash*, vi, 119.

157 Cf. Is. ii, 6 sqq. To the above two columns a third parallel column could easily be added listing the blessings secured by the functioning of the Temple in Jerusalem, or the existence of a "righteous man."

POSTSCRIPT 1967

I

To dispose, first of all, of the subject touched upon in the Introduction: the ceremony to which Robert Graves referred me is described by Apollonius Rhodius, the third-century B.C.E. Greek poet (who lived in Alexandria and on the Island of Rhodes), in his *Argonautica* (Book IV, lines 1717 ff.) as follows:

> Dawn came soon after and showed them the low island on which they had landed. They called it Anaphe, or Revelation, because Apollo had revealed it to them when they were benighted. In the shelter of some trees they consecrated ground and built him an altar in the shade, calling him the Lord of Light, whose beacon fire had lit them from afar. On that lonely coast they had little to offer him, but they offered what they could, with the result that when Medea's Phaeacian maids, who were accustomed to the rich sacrifices made in Alcinous' palace, saw them using water for libations on the burning logs, they could no longer refrain from laughing. The men, seeing the joke themselves, retaliated with some ribaldry, which was the signal for a light-hearted exchange of insult and repartee. This frolic of the Argonauts is commemorated by the island women, who chaff the men whenever they are sacrificing to Apollo, Lord of Light and protector of the Isle of Revelation.[1]

Were it not for the last sentence, one would not suspect that the events on Anaphe were nothing but the mythical validation of a ritual. But that last sentence gives the story away: it makes it clear that Graves was right in interpreting the passage as referring to a ceremony of water sacrifice accompanied by "lightheadedness." If a ritual is said to "commemorate" a past event, and especially an event from the early, mythical past, we can be sure that we are dealing with what could be called a myth-and-ritual syndrome. Unfortunately, Apollonius' account of the ritual on Anaphe is most laconic; but adding features from the myth one can reconstruct it as probably having consisted of the following rites:

1. The consecration of a piece of ground in the woods to Apollo.
2. Building of an altar in its midst, shaded by trees.
3. Lighting of fire on the altar.
4. Pouring of water upon the fire.
5. "Frolicking" between the men and the women touched off by the reaction of the latter to the water libation.

That the intent of this ritual was rain-making cannot be doubted. Points 1-4 are quite similar to the rites performed by Elijah in his rain-making competition with the prophets of Baal on Mount Carmel (see above, pp. 43-44), although Elijah did not light the wood on the altar he built, but waited until a fire from heaven consumed the sacrifice, burned the wood, and dried up the water (cf. 1 *Kings* 18:38). As to Point 5, the "frolicking," this certainly parallels closely the "lightheadedness" of the "Joy of the House of Water Drawing," and must have had the same underlying motivation.

My curiosity aroused, I read on in the *Argonautica* and found that the very next passage contained a myth bearing a certain resemblance to the Hebrew myth which tells how God began to create the world by casting a rock, the *Shetiyyah*-stone, into the midst of the primeval waters and how he built up the dry land around it (cf. above, pp. 57-58, 85-86, 101). In the *Argonautica* we read that the morning after the Argo sailed from Anaphe, Euphemus remembered a dream he had the night before:

> He was holding to his breast the lump of earth which the god [Triton] had given him and was suckling it with streams of white milk. The clod, small as it was, turned into a woman of virginal appearance; and in an access of passion he lay with her. When the deed was done, he felt remorse—she had been a virgin and he had suckled her himself. But she consoled him, saying in a gentle voice: 'My friend, I am of Triton's stock and the Nurse of your children; no mortal maid, but a Daughter of Triton and Libya. Give me a home with Nereus' Daughters in the sea near Anaphe, and I will reappear in the light of day in time to welcome your descendants!"

Upon hearing the dream, Jason interprets it unhesitatingly: "When you have thrown this clod of earth into the sea, the gods will make an island of it, and there your children's children are to live." Euphemus thereupon cast the clod into the sea, "and there grew up from it an island called Calliste" on which later the descendants of Euphemus lived.[2] In other words, what we have here is a typical origin-myth according to which the island of Calliste came into being in much the same manner in which the earth was said to have originated in the Hebrew myth of creaton (see above, p. 85).

By now I had almost reached the end of the *Argonautica,* and, reading on, I found that the next passage contained yet another example of the myth-and-ritual syndrome which had a parallel in Jerusalem. From Calliste the Argo sailed to Aegina (the last stop described in the *Argonautica*), and there the following rite was performed by her crew:

"They were short of water but wished to waste no time, as the wind still held. So they turned the business of watering into a game, racing one another to the spring, and back again with water to the ship. To this day the young Myrmidons of Aegina, carrying big jars full of water on their shoulders, race one another on the track with nimble feet."[3] Again, the commemorative races performed by the young Myrmidons of Aegina "to this day" indicate that the racing of the Argonauts is but the mythical validation of a ritual. Similarly in Jerusalem, young priests would race against one another up to the altar ramp in order to obtain the privilege of removing the ashes from the altar (cf. above, p. 73).

So much for parallels between the Jerusalem Temple ritual and its associated myths, and the myths and rituals of the Greek islands.

II

Now for those additional conclusions also referred to in the Introduction. Since these pursue the argument as presented in the body of the book, let me begin by recapitulating briefly the contents of the preceding six chapters.

At various levels of cultural and religious sophistication, man has developed sets of rituals performed with a view to influencing nature or natural forces and elements in his favor, by showing them what he expected them to do, or by cajoling them into fulfilling his wishes. The mythical correlate of this type of ritual is the attribution of human-like qualities, acts and behavior to the forces and elements of nature (Chapter I).

The greatest and most popular annual feast performed in the Second Temple of Jerusalem, the so-called "Joy of the House of Water Drawing," was a fine example of such a ritual. All the acts performed, and first and foremost the ceremony of water libation, had one central purpose: to bring about the onset of the autumnal rains on which depended the welfare and the very existence of the people. This purpose was subserved by the performance of a rich array of rites which symbolically but unmistakably indicated the natural phenomena they were supposed to bring about: favorable winds, thunder and lightning, and, most importantly, rain—good, rich and soft rain. One of the many rites performed was that of "lightheadedness," i.e. the indulgence in general sexual licence, whose ritual purpose was to induce the rain to copulate with the earth (Chapter II).

The mythological counterpart of these rituals was twofold: one type of myths told about the creation of the world, about the primal separation by God of the Upper Male Waters from the Lower Female Waters, and the ceaseless yearning of these two lustful elements to reunite: when it rained, their desire was actually achieved. The other told about the place and role of the Temple in the great divine cosmogonical and cosmological scheme: the Temple was the center of the whole universe, the navel of the earth; its foundations pressed down upon the Female Waters of Tehom, the primeval abyss, and its underground shafts reached down into its very depths. Also, the Temple was located on the highest peak on earth, very near heaven and facing its heavenly counterpart, the Sanctuary On High. Therefore, the ritual performed in the Temple, not only the ritual of Water Libation and its attendant ceremonies, but any ritual, had an unfailing, direct and immediate effect on the world, on the order and functioning of nature (Chapter III).

Moreover, the Temple symbolically represented the entire universe, and each and every rite performed in it affected that part or aspect of nature of which the rite itself was reminiscent. In fact, the function of the Temple was of such basic importance that the very existence of the entire world depended on it. According to the Talmud, the destruction of the Second Temple (70 C.E.) resulted in the gravest disturbances in the natural order, and thereafter the fertility of Palestine was reduced to a mere fraction of its former riches (Chapter IV).

However, the functioning of the natural order was believed to have depended not solely on the regular and precise performance of the Temple ritual, but also on the conduct of the people, particularly of its leaders, outside the sacred precincts. There existed, it was believed, an inner, a sympathetic connection between human conduct and the behavior of the natural forces. Sins, i.e. improper or illicit human acts, brought about improper or illicit occurrences in nature—it was in this view that the original, basic sanctions that made for religious conformity were anchored. In the earliest form of this religious imperative, the assumption was that the greatest of all sins was fornication, that is to say any form of illicit sexual intercourse, because by the inexorable law of sympathy such transgressions caused similar irregular interactions between the male and the female elements of nature: draughts, floods or other natural calamities which can, and in the days of Deluge actually did, destroy the world (Chapter V).

The other side of the coin was the complementary notion that a central personality, such as a patriarch, a king, or a pious and saintly man, had it in his power to influence the weather and thereby insure the well-being of his people, either directly, through the working of the same laws of sympathy, or indirectly, through the intermediacy of God. Either way, the merit possessed especially by the pious and righteous men was of such force that what they ordained had to come to pass. The culmination of this trend of thought was the idea that the coming of the Messiah would usher in a period of great fertility in the vegetable and animal kingdoms, and an era of peace and general welfare for mankind. Once this type of thinking was achieved, man was assumed to influence nature no longer through ties of magical sympathy, but through a spiritual and moral sympathy in which God served as the supreme catalyst between man and nature (Chapter VI).

III

So much for the original argument. In presenting it today, I see that I was too preoccupied with establishing, one by one, the points I considered essential, and, in order to do so, I felt I had to stress the similarities between the ancient Jewish myths and rituals and those of other ancient Near Eastern peoples. To strengthen my argument, I also considered it necessary on occasion to go beyond the confines of the ancient Near East, and to adduce myths or rituals from the modern Middle East and even from other parts of the world. The force of this cumulative evidence was deemed indispensable in order to establish the original meaning of the great ritual of water libation, and the basic significance of the myths connected with it and with the Jerusalem Temple in general. This led to an analysis of the ancient Jewish views on the relationship between sins and natural calamities, and of the role fulfilled by the king, the saintly man and the Messiah according to ancient Jewish view, in the threefold relationship between God and man, God and the world, and man and the world. And here, too, I concentrated, as I still believe I had to, on similarities between the ancient Hebrew-Jewish views and those of other ancient Near Eastern peoples. When the aim of a chapter was to show that the original purpose of the water libation in the Jerusalem Temple was to secure or induce the fall of the seasonal rains, the emphasis had to be on demonstrating that water libations for this avowed and explicity stated purpose were carried out by the functionaries of other temples in a manner closely resembling that of the Jerusalem Temple festivities. When the purpose of another chapter was to show that natural calamities were originally regarded by the Jews as a direct, almost automatic, effect of the commission of sins and that sins in this context primarily meant transgressions against the prevailing sexual code, it was inevitable that the argument should concentrate on similar views and beliefs held by other peoples, and that these similarities should be stressed. What I recognize today is that, after securing these points as firmly as possible, I should have gone one step further and tried to show the direction taken by the Talmudic Jewish world-view once it was forced to adjust to the new situation that developed when the Temple of Jerusalem was destroyed. Let me now, after a delay of two decades, attempt to supplement my original argument along these lines.

First of all, it should be pointed out that the early Palestinian teachers whose work is recorded in the Mishna, the two Talmuds and the rest of rabbinic literature, prepared the way for the Jewish people to live without its Temple and even without its country, by gradually shifting the emphasis from the role of the Temple and its ritual to that of man and his morality. To be sure, the very old and very basic idea that man and his behavior influence the functioning of nature, with or without the intermediacy of God, had not changed. But while in the older view the proper functioning of nature (and thus the well-being of Israel and of the world) depended on the correct performance of a sacrificial ritual, in the newer view the same effect came to be attributed to the moral qualities of individual men, not necessarily religious leaders or great luminaries of talmudic lore, but rather pious, saintly men, for whose sake, as the typical talmudic saying goes, the world exists.

This shift from Temple to man was correlated with that type of midrashic thought which elaborates on the idea that there is a structural as well as functional similarity between the world, the Temple and man. The Temple is simply the world on a small scale, and man is the world on an even smaller scale, a microcosm. But if this is so, it becomes immediately clear that the function formerly filled by the Temple could be taken over by man: there was no reason to suppose that the sympathy between the world and man was smaller or weaker in any way than that between the world and the Temple.

All this did not make the destruction of the Temple a smaller catastrophe, but it showed the road to survival as a religio-national community after the Exile, with man, the saintly individuum whose body was the new Temple of God, in control. The well-being of Israel now depended on, and was guaranteed by, the man of merit, whose powers were believed to be so great that even God had to obey him.

The change which can be observed in the character of this man of merit is also a process that requires more reflection and comment than I devoted to it twenty years ago. Today it seems to me that it is not enough to point out, as I did then, that the king at first was believed to possess quasi-magical powers over nature, and that these powers were successively attributed to types of leaders in whom the spiritual qualities gradually gained preponderance, such as the "whisperers," the "pious," the "*Tzaddiq*" (Righteous One) and the Messiah. In addition to this, it seems necessary to stress that the increasing emphasis on the moral qualities of these men enabled the community of Israel to wean itself emotionally and ideologically from the Temple ritual and to establish direct rapport between man and God, no longer predicated upon the intermediacy of a special descent group, that of the Aaronide priests and their helpers the Levites, and of a specially trained few individuals among them at that. Any man, even a Gentile, who possessed the rare spiritual-moral qualities of "saintliness," could now directly, by the sheer force of his inner qualities, influence God, bend Him to his will, and thus obtain whatever the people were in need of: ample rain, abundant crops, safety from enemy attack, and the like.

These ideational developments cushioned the blow which the destruction of the Temple of Jerusalem was to contemporary Jewry. For a thousand years, at least so it appeared in pious retrospect, the Jerusalem Temple had been not only the center of the universe, but with its meticulously performed ritual, the tangible guarantee of the survival of the world. Suddenly all this came to an end. The Temple went up in flames. Its ritual ceased abruptly. Yet the world did not go under, the forces of nature continued to function, and even the Jewish people lived on. All this was made possible, in the Jewish world-view developed by the sages, because the existence of the world, the functioning of nature, and the survival of the Jewish people had come to turn on a new pivot: the man of merits, who assumed varying characters—he was patriarch, king, "whisperer," "pious man," "man of faith," righteous, sage, student of the Law, and man of outstanding moral qualities. It is in this sense that, in place of the Temple, the *Tzaddiq,* or Righteous One, became the foundation of the world.

IV

Following the destruction of the Temple, the idea that the Sanctuary was the center of global fertility and that the Holy of Holies in it served as the nuptial chamber for God and the Matrona (cf. above, pp. 88-93) was extended in a different direction as well. To be sure, even after the Temple was gone, the spot on which it had stood retained its sanctity. In fact, since in later times it was no longer known exactly where the Holy of Holies had been located, the entire Temple Mount was placed out of bounds, and ever since that time pious Jews approached the holy site only as far as the famous Wailing Wall, which was but a part of the western outer boundary of the Temple courtyard. Moreover, and this is the significant development, the holiness of the Temple was extended over the entire city of Jerusalem, poetically referred to as Zion (although Zion was originally the name of the hill upon which the Temple itself stood), and Zion was personified as the Mother of the Jewish people.

The personification of the Holy City in the image of a woman has its roots in Biblical literature. In the historic books of the Bible one often encounters expressions such as "Heshbon and her daughters," "Ekron and her daughters," "Megiddo and her daughters." In other words, a big city was referred to as a mother, while the villages surrounding her and depending on her politically, were called "her daughters." We can mention only in passing that the same imagery underlies the Greek term for a big city, *metropolis,* literally "mother city."

In the poetic and prophetic books of the Bible, the peoples of the two Hebrew kingdoms, Israel and Judah, are often personified as women, and called e.g. Oholah and Oholibah,[4] or Daughter of Judah.[5]

In the Kingdom of Judah, whose capital, Jerusalem, was the center of all aspects of its life, the city, personified as a woman, came to stand for the entire country and people. Hence the frequent prophetic reference to "Daughter Jerusalem"[6] and "Daughter Zion,"[7] and to the adulterous Jerusalem who goes awhoring after all her neighbors.[8] Occasionally both names, Zion and Jerusalem, are used together in parallel fashion, as for instance when Isaiah addresses these words to Sennacherib king of Assyria in the name of God:

> The virgin daughter Zion
> Has despised and scorned you,
> The daughter Jerusalem
> Has shaken her head at you.[9]

The same imagery is found in Jeremiah: he speaks to the people of Jerusalem but addresses them as "daughter Jerusalem" and "virgin daughter Zion":

> What shall I take to witness for you?
> What shall I liken to you?
> O daughter Jerusalem!
> What shall I equal to you
> That I may comfort you
> O virgin daughter Zion![10]

Only rarely is the image of Zion as a mother used by the prophets. One such instance is found in Isaiah:

> As soon as Zion has travailed
> She brought forth her children.[11]

In the New Testament, both the earthly and heavenly Jerusalem are symbolically referred to as women and mothers.[12]

In the Apocrypha, the image of Mother Zion became stereotyped as that of the grieving widow, who is only kept alive by the hope that her husband and children would ultimately return to her. In the *Book of Baruch,* written shortly after the destruction of Jerusalem by Titus, Jerusalem herself addresses her children: ". . . I have seen the captivity of my sons and daughters . . . with joy did I nourish them, but sent them away with weeping and mourning. Let no man rejoice over me, a widow, and forsaken of many . . . Go your way O my children, go your way: for I am left desolate. I have put off the garment of peace and put upon me the sackcloth of my petition . . . I sent you out with mourning and weeping, but God will give you to me again with joy and gladness for ever . . .[13]

In the pseudepigraphic book *IV Ezra,* written in the early 2nd century C.E., Ezra is made to say: "I lifted up my eyes and saw a woman upon the right, and lo! she was mourning and weeping in a loud voice, and was much grieved in mind, and her clothes were rent and there were ashes upon her head. Then I dismissed my thoughts in which I had been preoccupied, and turned to her and said: Wherefore weepest thou? And why art thou grieved in thy mind? And she said unto me: Suffer me, my lord, to indulge in my sorrow and continue my grief . . ." When the woman tells him about the misfortunes that befell her, Ezra admonishes her to think rather of "Zion, the mother of all of us" who "is in great grief." The woman shortly becomes transformed into the appearance of a city, and the angel Uriel explains to Ezra: "This woman whom you saw is Zion, whom you now behold as a built-up city . . ."[14]

In the Syriac Apocalypse of Baruch, composed in the 3rd or 4th century C.E., Jeremiah's scribe is made to say: "Oh Lord, my Lord, have I come into the world for this purpose that I might see the evils of my mother? . . ."[15] And again: ". . . this mother is desolate, and her sons are led into captivity."[16]

In rabbinic literature, too, it became a commonplace to speak of "Mother Zion." The Targum (ca. 3rd century C.E.) introduces the idea into its paraphrase of a verse from the *Song of Songs* in the original text of which all that is said is "Thy mother was in travail with thee."[17] This is rendered in the Targum: "In that hour Zion, who is the mother of Israel, will give birth to her children."

A Midrash compiled in the 8th century C.E. contains the following passage:

> Jeremiah admonished his mother saying: My mother! You did not conceive me and bear me like all other mothers. Could it be that you committed adultery? If not, why don't you drink the bitter water?[18] How do we know that Jeremiah spoke thusly? From the words, "Thou hadst a harlot's forehead, thou didst refuse to be ashamed"[19] [which Jeremiah addressed to Judah]. When his mother heard this, she said: Why do you accuse me, without any reason? He answered: I was not speaking about you, my mother, nor was I prophesying concerning you. It was of Zion and Jerusalem that I said that she adorned her daughters, clothed them in crimson silk, and crowned them with gold. For the robbers will come and despoil them, "Tou, that art despoiled, what doest thou that thou clothest thyself with scarlet . . ."[20]

In another passage, the same Midrash brings Jeremiah face to face with the grieving Mother Zion:

> Jeremiah said: When I went up to Jerusalem I raised my eyes and saw a woman sitting on top of the mountain. Her clothes were black, her hair dishevelled, and she was seeking consolation. And I, too, was weeping and hoping that somebody would comfort me. I approached her, and spoke to her: If you are a woman, talk to me, and if you are a spirit, get away from here! She answered: Don't you recognize me? I am she who had seven sons. Their father left and went overseas, and while I was bemoaning his departure, a messenger came and told me that the house had collapsed and killed my seven sons. Now I don't know whom to mourn and over whom to tear my hair! I said to her: You are not worse off than my Mother Zion who has been turned into a pasture for the beasts of the field. She replied: I am your Mother Zion, I am the mother of seven, as it is written, "She that hath borne seven languisheth."[21]

Other legends tell about the vain efforts of the prophets to comfort the desolate Mother Jerusalem:

> In that hour all the prophets returned and gathered and went to Jerusalem to comfort her. The Holy One, blessed be He, said to them: Whom should you comfort first, Me or Jerusalem? If a son dies, is it not his father whom people comfort? If a house is burned down, is it not its owner whom people comfort? How much more am I in need of being comforted first? Nevertheless, go and comfort her. All of them gathered and went to her. When she saw them, she said: Go hence, I don't need the consolation of my sons. Thereupon they returned to the Holy One, blessed be He, and said to Him: Master of the Universe! She does not accept our consolation! He said to them: The proper thing to do is that nobody but I myself should go and comfort her . . .[22]

In other sources, detailed accounts are given of the words addressed by each prophet to the grief-stricken Jerusalem, and of the words she quoted from the books of the same prophets in her refusal to be comforted by them.[23] Only when her husband, God, will return to her, will the Matrona, Jerusalem, be again filled with rejoicing.[24]

It is in keeping with this idea of Zion personified as the mother of Israel that she is enumerated among the seven originally barren women who miraculously gave birth to children—the other six being Sarah, Rebekkah, Rachel, Leah, the wife of Manoah and Hannah.[25]

From the midrashic lore one can thus distill the following features:

1. Zion (Jerusalem) is the mother of Israel.
2. Mother Zion is the spouse of God.
3. Mother Zion is identical with the Matrona.
4. The Temple was the home of God and the Matrona.
5. When the Temple was destroyed, God the husband left His wife, the Matrona, and went "overseas."
6. Mother Zion was bereft also of her children, who went into exile.
7. But her children will return to her,
8. As will her husband, God.

A symbolic figure closely related in midrashic sources to Mother Zion is *Knesset Yisrael,* the Community of Israel. A mournful, motherly figure, the Community of Israel addresses herself to God in a lengthy discourse in which she laments her fate, the destruction of her home, the Temple, in which she once dwelled and into which God would send down His Shekhina (i.e. personified Presence) to rest on her.[26] A few centuries later, in Kabbalistic literature, the figure of the Matronit, the female aspect of the deity, was substituted for the Community of Israel, and both her joyful midnightly union with God the King in the Holy of Holies of the Jerusalem Temple, and her anguish over having lost home and husband, were described in considerable detail, as illustrated by the brief excerpt quoted above on pages 92-93.[27]

At the same time, the mystical identity of the Matronit with Zion was also preserved in Kabbalistic writings. The Zohar contains numerous passages describing the union between God and Zion, one of which, termed by Gershom Scholem an "unusually daring homily,"[28] reads as follows:

> The male member is the completion of the entire body [of God the King] and it is called *Yesod* (Foundation), and this is the feature that delights the Female, and all the desire of the Male for the Female which is in this Yesod penetrates the Female at the place called Zion, for there is the covered place of the Female, like unto the womb in a woman. This is why the Lord of Hosts is called *Yesod.* It is written: "For the Lord hath chosen Zion, He hath desired it for His habitation"[29]—when the Matronit separated from Him. And she unites with the King face to face on the Sabbath eve, and both become one body. Then the Holy One, blessed be He, seats Himself on His throne, and all cry, His Name is complete, the Holy Name, blessed is His Name forever and ever! . . . When the Matronit unites with the King all the worlds become blessed and all are in a state of great joy . . . and the Matronit becomes intoxicated with joy and blessed in the place that is called the Holy of Holies here below, as it is written, "For there the Lord commanded the blessing."[30]

Here Mount Zion appears as the *mons veneris* of the Matronit into which the generative organ of God the King, driven by a mighty desire, penetrates. In the mystical scheme of the universe created by the Kabbalists, Zion thus became the focal point, the spot in which the actual union of God and the Matronit (who here is not merely the female aspect of the deity but also symbolic of Israel, the people, and Israel, the land) takes place, and from where, consequently, blessings emanate into the entire world.

At the same time, the concept of Zion as the grieving mother of Israel and the forsaken spouse of God also remained alive in Kabbalistic circles. The Zohar is replete with references to the Matronit, identified with Zion, abandoned by her husband, God the King, and wailing amidst the ruins of the Temple. Three centuries after the Zohar, the dramatic encounter with Mother Zion, attributed by the Midrash to Jeremiah, was relived by the Safed Kabbalist Rabbi Abraham Halevi—whether under the influence of that Midrash or as the spontaneous re-emergence of a quasi-Jungian archetypal mythologem, we cannot tell. In any case, the pious chronicler of the Safed Kabbalist circle, Shlimel Dresnitz, describes in one of his epistles written shortly after 1600 that Rabbi Abraham Halevi—who, incidentally, was considered a reincarnation of Jeremiah—following a severe illness went to Jerusalem, where he spent three days in solitude, fasting and weeping, and then betook himself to the Wailing Wall to pray. When he finished his prayers, he lifted up his eyes, and saw a woman on top of the wall, with her back toward him, dressed in clothes of mourning. Rabbi Abraham fell on his face and cried: "Mother, Mother! Mother Zion, woe to me that I must see you thus!" And he tore his hair and beat his head against the wall until he lost consciousness and collapsed. When he came to, he found that the Shekhina had taken his head between her knees, she wiped away his tears and spoke words of comfort to him: "Abraham, my son, be comforted, for your children will return home to their country."[31]

Thus the image of Zion the Mother, identical with the Shekhina, the female aspect of the deity, awaiting the return of her children, which was to signal the return of her husband as well, remained alive in Jewish consciousness. It is in this sense that the old dependence that had riveted the attention of the Jewish people to the Temple became expanded and developed into a bond that tied the people to Mother Zion, and into an unquenchable yearning to be clasped again to her motherly bosom. The Man-Temple relationship became supplanted by a Man-Motherland relationship, which was more permanent and more solid because it did not depend on concrete artifacts, man-made structures and ritual performances, but was anchored purely and solely in the realm of profound feeling, in the unshakable certainty of emotional and ideational realities. At the same time, and this is more significant, the relationship was humanized: the people's yearning was no longer for a building, however sacrosanct, but for a human image, the image of the mother. The mother-image of Zion and the father-image of the Tzaddiq, the almost omnipotent saintly, pious man, thus became the two mirrors in which the people could perceive God and view the workings of His will, if not with understanding, at least with acquiescence.

FOOTNOTES

1 New Translation by E. V. Rieu, Penguin Classics, 1959, p. 193.
2 Rieu's transl., pp. 193-94.
3 Rieu, pp. 194-95.
4 *Ezekiel* 23:4 ff.
5 *Lamentations* 2:2.
6 *Habat Y'rushalayim, Lamentations* 2:13; or *Bat Y'rushalayim, Zephaniah* 3:14.
7 *Isaiah* 1:8, *Jeremiah* 4:31.
8 *Ezekiel* 16 and 23. It should be mentioned here that the prophets referred also to other peoples by the epithet "daughter," e.g. "Daughter of Egypt" (*Jeremiah* 46:11, 19, 24), "Daughter of Babylon" (*Jeremiah* 50:42; 51:33; *Psalms* 137:8) "Daughter of Edom" (*Lamentations* 4:21). In view of this usage it is remarkable that the expression "Daughter of Israel" is never used.
9 2 *Kings* 19:21, and *Isaiah* 37:22.
10 *Lamentations* 2:13.
11 *Isaiah* 66:8; cf. *Micah* 4:10.
12 *Matthew* 23:37; *Galatians* 4:26.
13 *Baruch* 4:8 ff.; Charles ed. I:592 ff.
14 IV *Ezra* 9:38-10:57, Charles II:603-08.
15 Syriac *Apocalypse of Baruch* 3:1 ff., Charles II:482.
16 *Op. cit.* 10:16, Charles, II:486.
17 *Song* 8:5.
18 The potion given, according to *Numbers* 5:12-31, to a woman suspected of adultery.
19 *Jeremiah* 3:3.
20 *Jeremiah* 4:30; Pesiqta Rabbati, ed. Friedmann, 129a.
21 *Jeremiah* 15:9; Pesiqta Rabbati, ed. Friedmann, p. 131b.
22 *Yalqut Shimoni, Lamentations,* §1031.
23 Pesiqta DiR. Kahana, ed. S. Buber, pp. 127b-129a, ed. Mandelbaum, pp. 273 ff.; Pesiqta Rabbati, ed. Friedmann, 138b-139a; *Yalqut Shimoni* Isaiah 443.
24 Pesiqta diR. Kahana, ed. Buber, p. 147b, ed. Mandelbaum, p. 328.
25 Pesiqta diR. Kahana, ed. Buber, p. 141a; ed. Mandelbaum, 310.
26 Cf. *Lamentations Rabbati,* Introduction 24.
27 A detailed treatment of the Matronit as a female deity in Kabbalistic thought is found in my study "Matronit: the Goddess of the Kabbala," *History of Religions,* vol. 4, no. 1, Summer 1964, pp. 53-68, and in my forthcoming book *The Hebrew Goddess.*
28 Gershom Scholem, *Von der mystischen Gestalt der Gottheit,* Zurich: Rhein Verlag, 1962, p. 139.
29 *Psalms* 132:13.
30 *Psalms* 133:3; *Zohar* III:296a-b, Idra Zutta.

31 S. Assaf, *Kobetz 'al Yad,* Minora Manuscripta Hebraica, vol. XIII. ed. by Mekitze Nirdamim, 1940, p. 123; as quoted by G. Scholem, *op. cit.* p. 187.

INDEX